...an Raaltes and

Brownsea Island 1901 to 19...

> Brownsea is a winsome place,
> Full of beauty, charm and grace;
> Everything to please the eye
> And fill the heart with ecstacy.
>
> Watery dune and pine-clad hill,
> Narcissus and daffodil,
> Turreted castle near the sea,
> Beautiful church in grassy lea.
>
> Lover of beauty, bend the knee
> To this beauteous spot in the silver sea.
> A spot unrivalled, of beauty rare.
> Remain here for ever, free from care!
> With happy memories of Brownsea. *M. Pleass*
> *Easter 1937.*

A WINSOME

by

PETER MOORE

Dedicated to the memory of

ALAN MARSH

founder of the National Trust Archive Team on Brownsea Island

POOLE HISTORICAL TRUST

This volume is published by the Poole Historical Trust whose primary aims are the promotion of research into and the publication of works on the history and life of Poole and the surrounding area.

Previous Publications
The Pride of Poole, 1688-1851
An Album of Old Poole
Mansions and Merchants of Poole and Dorset
Brownsea Islander
Poole and World War II
A Portfolio of Old Poole
Ebb-Tide at Poole
History of the Town of Poole, 1839 (reprint)
The Sydenhams of Poole (booklet)
Art in Poole and Dorset
Victorian Poole
Poole after World War II 1945-1953
D-Day Poole (booklet)
The Spirit of Poole 1953-1963
Lifeboatmen Never Turn Back
Schools of Old Poole
Poole's Pride Regained 1964-1974
Poole Was My Oyster
For Nature, Not Humans
Hengistbury Head - The Whole Story
The RMYC 1905-2005 (Private Publication)
A Pint of Poole Good Ale

Edited by Terry McDonald
Designed by Andrew S Arnold.
Production by Graphic Editions, Poole.
Printed and bound in Great Britain by The Baskerville Press, Salisbury, Wiltshire.

CONTENTS

List of Illustrations

Preface & Acknowledgements

I am grateful for the memoirs lodged in the National Trust's Brownsea Island Archive. I am sure that there were periods of sadness, but friendship and support for each other from all those living on the Island predominates in the period 1901 to 1925.

Reference has been made to unpublished childhood memories and photographs and newspaper cuttings

- Daisy Chapman (née Toms), Gwen Jennings (née Toms), collected and added to by 'Chappie' (Melvin) Chapman as *Brownsea Toms*
- *Four Generations of the Dean Family 1840-1927* by William A Dean
- *Brownsea Island and the Castle* by C T Biggs
- Memories of Dorothy Carr (née Pool) from her daughter Betty Ann Branson
- Audio tapes of Louise Brayley (née Campbell) and George Blackmore interviewed by Kim and Beryl Parkyn
- Autograph book and information on May and William (Tresco) Brown from Sean Pedley
- Information on the Church its records and Island inhabitants collected by Dot Orchard and collated by her daughter Janet Mellors
- 1927 Sale documents from Mr T Fox, retired director of Fox & Sons
- Ron Worthington - photographs and cuttings
- Newspaper cuttings from the Bournemouth Echo
- Bob Briggs - Latin translation
- Letters to Councillor Saunders donated by Peter Saunders
- Photographs from Sue Sieger
- Dr Terry McDonald for advice and the final edit
- Poole Historical Trust for their advice and guidance

Book references:

Pages from My Life by Margherita Lady Howard de Walden (née van Raalte)
My Father Marconi by Degna Marconi
A History of Brownsea Island by Bugler and Drew
Earls have Peacocks by 9th Lord Howard de Walden
Nouveau Riches by J Mordaunt Crook
Brownsea Islander by Jack Battrick
The Farmers Tour through England by Arthur Young, 1771

References from:

Local History Centre, Poole Waterfront Museum
Dorset History Centre, Dorchester
The Dorset County Museum, Dorchester

Considerable assistance has been given by other members of the Archive Team:

- Alan Marsh who collected census returns, school details, family trees, and photographs
- John Argent who has masterminded the computer indexing and collected information on maps, and legal documents
- Brian Ellis who edited, and suggested many improvements to, the penultimate draft

The book would not have been written without the help of my typist, Sheila Argent, and the support and encouragement from my wife, Jean.

Editors Note

Sadly, Peter Moore died before the Trust was able to complete the production process for this book. The Trustees extend condolences to his widow, family and friends.

Castle, Brownsea Island

Brownsea Island before 1901

Brownsea Island is the largest of Poole Harbour's five islands, being one and a half miles long, three quarters of a mile wide, and covering 560 acres. The harbour is reputed to be the second largest harbour in the world. Brownsea lies towards the entrance to the harbour and one of its earliest roles was to be part of the defences for the towns and settlements within that body of water. However, it has also been a family home, a country estate, a business venture and a retreat from the rest of the world. It was as clearly being used as a retreat when it made its first appearance in a written document for, in 1015, it was described as having no buildings except for a chapel. In the late tenth and early eleventh centuries its sole inhabitant was a hermit monk from Cerne Abbas.

By the sixteenth century the harbour had within its shores one of southern England's major ports. Poole, including Hamworthy, had developed steadily since the thirteenth century and during the reign of Henry VIII Brownsea Island became an important part of its defences. A blockhouse was built to house the soldiers who manned the cannons overlooking the harbour entrance. These were there to prevent attack by the French and Spanish and eventually became the responsibility of the Poole authorities. Overall control of the island remained with the Crown but during the reign of Elizabeth I, Sir Christopher Hatton (1540-1591) was granted Corfe Castle by the Queen. One of her favourites, he was known as the 'Dancing Chancellor'. Sir Christopher was also appointed as Admiral of Purbeck and Brownsea Island fell under his jurisdiction, and he was one of a number of men who, in the sixteenth and seventeenth centuries, were granted possession of Brownsea by the crown.

In the second half of the seventeenth century Brownsea Island appears to have become private property, for John Sydenham, Poole's first 'proper' historian, records it as being owned by Sir Robert Clayton. His heirs sold it, 'before 1722', for £300 to a man called William Benson (1682-1754), who was Auditor of the Imprest but became better known as 'Mad' Benson after making some questionable architectural decisions in London. Among his possessions was a large collection of books and there are tales of orgies and black magic rituals during his ownership of Brownsea. It is said that, during a fit of depression, he piled all his books upon the beach and burnt them. He was one of a number of owners to make their mark upon the island by improving the original blockhouse and turning it into a castle. Additional floors and annexes were added, using a variety of colours with brick and stone.

In the eighteenth century, it was owned by wealthy landowner Humphrey Sturt of Critchel House near Wimborne, followed by his son Henry Charles Sturt. Like so many

18th Century Castle on Empress of Catherine of Russia's Wedgwood dinner service

other landowners during this period, he instigated a great deal of change. Trees were planted, ornamental gardens were laid out, the poor soil was manured and crop rotation was introduced so that various crops were cultivated. Peat cutting created the freshwater East and West Lakes. Cottages were also built along the Island's quay for the Coastguards. Brownsea's strategic position at the entrance to Poole Harbour was still important. A substantial house, the Villano, known earlier as the Villino, part of which now houses the National Trust café, was built for the senior Coastguard Officer. Sir Charles Chad bought the Island in 1817, and he continued the extensions to the Castle and the development of ornamental gardens and parks. Seymour's (or Seymers) Cottage was built near the northern shore for a gamekeeper who reared pheasants.

The island was bought by a former diplomat, Sir Augustus Foster, in 1845 for £14,000 and he lived there for three years. He became ill during his time on Brownsea and, like a previous owner, had fits of depression and committed suicide by cutting his throat.

In 1853, Foster's widow Albinia, sold Brownsea for £13,000 to a man who was to literally leave his mark on the island. He was Colonel William Waugh, formerly of the 10th Regiment of Hussars and a director of the London and Eastern Bank, who thought he had bought a real bargain. This was because he believed the island to contain huge amounts of china clay and envisaged making millions of pounds profit by using it to manufacture high class tableware. This made a certain amount of sense for there was a growing demand for such products by the owners of England's many country houses.

With such potentially fantastic profits to be made, Colonel Waugh embarked on a building spree. He borrowed money from the London and Eastern Bank and began transforming the island into an industrial community. At the western end of the island, as far away from the castle as it was possible to get, he had a 200 by 60 feet three storey building constructed, as well as a drying shed, kilns, and a tramway to another, smaller pottery (albeit 150 feet long) and two piers. He built a farm, a village he named Maryland (after his wife) to accommodate some of his workforce which quickly reached over 200 men. He built a church, St Mary's, of course, and a vicarage, which is now known as the Villa on the Dorset Wildlife Trust's Nature Reserve. He also completed a wall around the mudflats of St. Andrew's Bay, now the lagoon, and built a windmill to pump out the water in order to increase the area of pasture land on the island. His intention was to make the population of about three hundred self-sufficient. Apart from the pottery and Maryland village, all the buildings remain and the lagoon (part of the Dorset Wildlife Trust's Nature Reserve) now has its water depth controlled by a diesel pump. This has recently been supplemented by a wind pump in order to maintain the shallow depth.

The Colonel clearly enjoyed his new role as a benevolent entrepreneur and set out to make Brownsea Castle a major part of the area's social circuit. In January 1856 the Poole and Southwestern Herald reported on the 'Annual Ball at Branksea Castle' where the Colonel and his lady had entertained the more eminent members of the local population, including several members of the Guest family of Canford Manor.

Unfortunately for the Colonel, his grand scheme was based upon false information. The Island's clay was not, as he had believed, suitable for the production of fine porcelain but was, instead, only of use for what was, ironically, the opposite end of the market, the

The Castle, after the Fire 1896

production of sewage pipes. It was also to have been used for producing tiles, bricks and cheap terracotta but, although there was a huge demand for these in a rapidly industrialising Britain, the costs of transporting them to the mainland meant that they could not compete with local products. In 1857 Colonel Waugh and his wife suddenly left England for Spain, owing at least £350,000, with some reports suggesting it may have been in excess of £600,000.

For several years the mortgagees tried to sell the island for £50,000 but were unsuccessful. Eventually, in 1873, it was sold to the Rt. Hon. George Augustus Frederick

Cavendish Bentinck, MP, who set up a company to produce, according to its advertisements, 'Salt-glazed stoneware, drain pipes, siphons, gullies, traps, inverts, terra cotta chimney pots and chimney cores, fire bricks, garden edgings etc.' The company struggled on for thirteen years, providing work for over 200 people, and boasting that it had been awarded the 'First and only Prize awarded by the Sanitary Institute of Great Britain', but geography was against it and it closed down in 1885. Cavendish Bentinck was a collector of Venetian and other Italian *objects d'art* and named the gardens near the Villa 'Venetia Park', after his daughter Venetia, and gave Italian names to the cottages near the castle. He is buried in the Island's church-yard and his grave is marked by an Italian well-head.

In 1890 the island was bought by a Captain Kenneth Balfour, a wealthy landowner who became Tory Member of Parliament for Christchurch from 1900 to 1906, but because of his wife's ill-health this gentleman and his family were absent from it for long periods. In 1896 a disastrous fire had gutted the castle and although Balfour had it restored, he put the island up for sale in 1899*. In 1901 it was bought by a London based businessman Charles van Raalte, and Brownsea Island was about to enjoy one of the happiest periods in its long history.

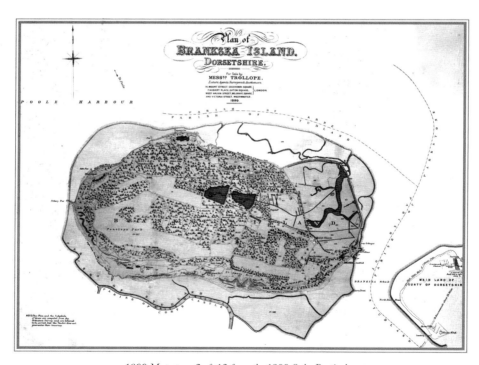

1899 Map, page 2 of 12 from the 1899 Sales Particulars

* *Appendix A 1899 Sales Literature*

The van Raalte Family

As their name suggests, the van Raaltes were of Dutch origin and the family owned a prosperous cigar making company. It was the grandfather of Charles van Raalte who inadvertently contributed to Brownsea's 'renaissance' for he gave each of his sons the equivalent of £1,500 when they reached the age of sixteen and told them to, 'go out into the world and seek your fortune.' One of his sons, Marcus, chose England as the place to make his fortune and moved to Birmingham. Marcus later moved to London and became a member of the Stock Exchange.

During his time in Birmingham he married, in 1853, Ramah Mendez da Costa, a lady of Portuguese descent. Four years later their only son, Charles, was born. His parents educated him at home and he developed an interest in early musical instruments,

Photo of Mr and Mrs van Raalte their children and Charles' parents
(Photo by kind permission of East Ayrshire Arts and Museum)

Margherita (left) and Noel van Raalte ready for Sailing

Gwen van Raalte

something that stayed with him throughout his life and he built up a considerable collection. As an adult, he followed his father into the Stock Exchange and had a number of business interests in the Far East.

Charles was 30 when he married the 24 year old Florence Clow in 1887. Their daughter Margherita later claimed that she was 'the twelfth of eighteen children and was considered the prettiest and most talented.' She had studied at the Royal Academy School of Art and through her portrait painting she made contacts with London 'high society'. She and Charles had met at her studio. Their marriage produced three children, Noel, born in 1889 and known within the family as Nony, his sister Margherita a year later and after another three years, Gwen. The children were born at their grandparents' house, 8 Kensington Palace Gardens, where Ramah was known as Little Granny.

Charles and Florence van Raalte were active members of London society, being part of the set that revolved around the Prince of Wales (the future King Edward VII) and which included several prominent Jewish families such as the Levitas, the Rothschilds and the Sassoons. When Charles and Florence lived at 46, Grosvenor Square, one of the most desirable addresses in London, among their neighbours was the Queen's financial advisor, Sir Ernest Cassell. Like the van Raaltes, Cassell was eventually to have a seaside residence in Poole, for he bought a house at Branksome Dene. Thanks to Little Granny's connections with Spain and Portugal, the van Raaltes also numbered members of the European nobility among their friends and acquaintances.

Much of our knowledge of this period in the lives of Charles and Florence van Raalte was provided by their daughter Margherita and she remembered a number of instances from her childhood. On one occasion she laughed when a nanny was bathing young Nony in a tin bath in the nursery. As a punishment the nanny shut Margherita in a cupboard and this resulted in her having a phobia about bogeymen lurking in dark places for many years after. One attempt at counteracting her phobia was to name her Shetland pony 'Bogey'. The influence nannies within upper class English households at this time was strong and it was a German one that Margherita remembered with particular distaste. She maintained that eventually the whole world would speak German and write in German whenever Margherita protested about having to learn the language.

When quite young Margherita contracted diphtheria and nearly died. As a last resort the doctors tried a new discovery, the anti-diphtheria vaccine, and she recovered. During the early stages of the illness she had been given a large collection of dolls and dolls' clothes and was most upset when they had to be burnt in case they harboured diphtheria germs.

When Margherita was about six years old, she had been given a tiny violin by 'Little Granny' and this became (after her doll) her favourite possession. Whenever she misbehaved, her violin was put on top of a cupboard for the remainder of the week. She never learned to play the instrument but, at the age of fourteen and now living on Brownsea Island, she persuaded her mother to allow her to have violin lessons. She may well have been influenced by the fact that she was surrounded by her father's collection of musical instruments, the largest in the British Isles. She was an enthusiastic pupil, for at Boarding school she would get up an hour earlier than the other girls in order to practise, but by then she was too old to acquire the finger technique that was essential for the more proficient violinists.

Before Boarding school, Noel and Margherita went to a morning school 'just around the corner' from the Grosvenor Square house which was run by two sisters. One of these two ladies, Miss Anna Patterson, was to be involved with the van Raalte children at a later date.

When Ramah died, Marcus van Raalte exchanged his large home at 46, Grosvenor Square for the one that Charles and Florence owned at 40, Brook Street. Later they moved to Aldenham Abbey near Watford. This was their first step towards becoming 'landed gentry' for the Abbey had been built as a country house in 1801 and had grounds of 400 acres, complete with a nine hole golf course and its lawns were used as a meeting place by the local hunt. Whilst living there, the children's nursery governess was one of the sisters from the London day school, Miss Anna Patterson. She was known as Miss Patty and slept in a bed between those of Noel and Margherita. Her remedy for preventing colds was to pour two cans of cold water down their backs each morning! It did not work as the children still caught colds and bronchitis.

Charles sold Aldenham Abbey shortly before buying Brownsea, and leased a house in Brighton. By this time Noel was at a private Boarding school but during the holidays the children enjoyed the many delights available in that seaside town. Margherita remembered going to the theatre and to concerts on the pier with two members of the Spanish royal family, Prince Alphonso (whom she knew as Ali) and Prince Luis. Their mother was the Infanta Eulalia of Spain, aunt to King Alphonso XIII.

Noel, unlike his sister, was not interested in horses or carriages although he later became keen on fast boats and motor cars. When W.O. Bentley manufactured his first car, he gave it to Noel so that he could 'show it off' in London. His father, Charles, bought a car of his own before the move to Brownsea. It was a $3\frac{1}{2}$ horse-power, two seater, open top Benz and came complete with a 'crypto.' This was similar to a short poker and was used to anchor the car to the road when stationary although on some slopes, this form of brake was not effective. The car had a 'violent first gear' and could be driven over fields and could jump culverts. Some fifty years later it was still functioning and was in the London to Brighton Rally. It was never taken to Brownsea.

Margherita, though, was driving a coach and a pair of horses when she was ten years old. Her father, of course, sat beside her on a box seat. The wooden blocks of London streets were awash with dirt, slush and horse droppings and as a warning at corners, a groom on a carriage would blow his highly polished horn. Sometimes they would skid when turning a corner and the horses would fall, tipping over the carriage. Crossing sweepers would earn tips from pedestrians for clearing a path through the muck.

After 1901, life in London was to be only part-time – possibly leasing a house for short periods – when Charles and Florence van Raalte bought a new and unique estate, in Southern England known as Brownsea Island.

Purchasing Brownsea Island

In 1890 Brownsea Island had been bought by Captain (later Major) Kenneth Balfour for £36,000, a price that included most of the objets d'art collected by the previous owner, the Rt. Hon. George Cavendish Bentinck.

In July 1899 Captain Balfour decided to sell. He put the island up for auction and, as one of the auctioneers' clerks, a Mr Wyatt, was walking upstairs to the room where the auction would take place, he was spoken to by a man with a black beard. This unknown gentleman asked Wyatt if, in the event of his (the stranger) being called out of the room during the auction, would Wyatt bid up to £38,000 for the island on behalf of Gordon's Hotel Ltd. Mr Wyatt did what he had been asked and achieved the purchase, but when Gordon's Hotel was contacted, they had no knowledge of the encounter and sent a telegram stating that the auctioneers had been, "Victims of a cruel and wicked hoax.". The solicitors and auctioneers assumed that someone had been trying to gauge how much interest there was in the island's sale and how much it would sell for. The reserve price had been £36,000.

In April 1900 Balfour's solicitors received a letter from a firm called George Trollope and Sons offering £20,000 for Brownsea, plus £500 for valuation items, on behalf of "Mr van Raalte of Aldenham Abbey." This offer was not accepted. Nine months later Balfour's solicitors received a letter dated 8 January 1901 from Charles van Raalte who was currently living at 87, Marine Parade, Brighton and which announced that his father "declines to have anything to do with the purchase of Branksea"* and that he (Charles) "makes a higher offer of £25,000." It is assumed that Charles had hoped his father would help him in purchasing the island.

Charles' offer was based on the auctioneers' details from 1899 along with the valuation of the electrical fittings, blinds, cannons, hurdles, live and dead stock, hay, straw, farm implements, garden tools, fitted book cases, wire netting, boats and launch. The sale agreement on what constitutes "the extras" on a house sale can be difficult and in the case of Brownsea Island, with its castle, farm and cottages, some of which were occupied, it was a nightmare. The statues and objets d'art bought by Cavendish Bentinck, pictures, peat-digging contracts, farm implements, etc. were the subject of considerable correspondence over a long period, which continued after Charles van Raalte had taken possession of the estate. There were stables on the mainland, at Sandbanks, which had been bought by Captain Balfour from Lord Wimborne, and these were included in the

* The island was still know as Branksea at this time

Musical Instruments displayed on the Wall in the 1927 Sale

main purchase price. In January 1901 it was agreed that van Raalte would pay £27,500 (several publications wrongly report the price as lower) for the island, the money being paid in two parts, the first in March 1901. The second instalment was to be paid in September at 0.5% above bank rate interest. In March 1901 £2,750 (representing a 10% deposit) was paid and contracts were exchanged for possession that month. Still more exchanges of correspondence took place, including whether or not the pony carriage was included in the main sale, and that the pheasants should be left to breed.

After the fire of 1896, Captain Balfour had reduced the number of people working and living on the island and, in 1899, when he decided to sell he reduced the staff still

Above: Harpsichord
Italian C16 (Appendix
Lot 1024)

Harpsichord 1630 by
Ruckers (Lot 1904)

Piano by Pape, Paris, C19 (Lot 1925)

*Lutina Bergonzi dated 1755
(not in the 1927 sale)*

*Portrait of a Young Lady in Blue Dress by
Sir Peter Lely*

further. The census taken in April 1901, before the van Raalte family had taken up residence, shows that the Castle was occupied by the 50 year old housekeeper, Victoria Bluitt. She was recorded as being married and being born in Shoreditch, London. The other occupant was the fifteen year old housemaid Mary McKay from Inverness, Scotland. In total 66 people lived on the island, 23 of them under ten years old. The census omits

18

Castle Drawing Room

Tapestry Panel (right hand folded corner because of obstruction on the wall)

the occupiers of one of the houses in Venetia Park who were away on census night. Twenty years earlier, in 1881, there had been 270 people living on Brownsea.

When the time came for the van Raaltes to occupy their new home, Charles' wife Florence, thought her daughter Margherita too quiet a child who needed "bringing out" so she, at the age of eleven, was sent with her father to assist with the move. It was, inevitably, a massive undertaking. Mr van Raalte and his daughter went by train to Poole

Another interior of the Castle.

and then took a twenty minute boat ride to Brownsea by a Harvey's boat. One witness, an islander named William Dean, said that there were 33 railway truck loads of furniture brought to Poole and then taken across to the island, using a cattle barge pulled by a launch. Two trips were made each day and on arrival at the Island Quay the trucks were put on to a horse drawn four wheeled undercarriage to be taken to the castle. Four islanders assisted in this process, the boatmen Tom Dean and Tom Biggs, the electrician Mr Cobb and the head estate carpenter, Mr Campbell. In addition to the furniture there were pictures, books, and Charles' precious musical instruments which included three pianos, a pianola, a pipe organ and an electric piano which played polkas, waltzes and tunes from Gilbert and Sullivan comic operas.

Charles van Raalte did indeed build up Margherita's self-confidence. He never laughed at her mistakes and even taught her to perform cartwheels, a skill that she was able to demonstrate in adult life to her own children on the ramparts of Chirk Castle, in the Welsh Marches, after her marriage to Thomas Evelyn Scott-Ellis, 8th Baron Howard de Walden in 1912. Having moved into Brownsea Castle, Margherita and her father initially used only one small ground floor room where they apparently lived for several weeks on a diet of chicken and stewed fruit. Meals were prepared for them by a girl caretaker, presumably the fifteen year old Mary McKay.

Four-Leaf Screen (Lot 2193) with four original hunting paintings by H Alken dated 1827.
Lower part are four original scenes by an unknown artist

Young Christian Biggs, whose father worked for three Brownsea owners, described the castle in great detail and with obvious awe:

> *"There were 70 to 80 rooms, including 22 best rooms with dressing rooms. There was a bathroom in each wing, and some bedrooms had their own bathroom. There were 'as many windows and glass doors as there are days in the year.' Floors were published with beeswax. There was an electric lift serving all floors. The island electricity generating station was near the quay with one steam and one gas engine. The gas engine could also be used for pumping water from the sea. The telephone cable had been laid along the sea bed to the castle. There were fire appliances and sea water could be pumped as far as the farm buildings."*

CT Biggs who had collected the family memories reported that:

> *"the castle had beautiful surroundings of lawns, flower and rose beds and herbaceous borders. Roses climbed old ropes suspended from poles. The private castle pier was flanked by twin towers which included bathing (i.e. changing) rooms and was connected to the garden by a long covered corridor. A large number of marble statues on green marble bases were arranged on either side of the corridor. On the terraces were very old cannons with cannon balls. Inside the castle there were four suits of armour and, very old fire arms, revolvers, shields and helmets were suspended on walls."*

Christian Biggs reminiscences ended with one painful memory – the swarms of mosquitoes that appeared each summer!

Edwardian Elegance

Washing Tubs and Box Mangle (photo 1962)
Below: Laundry Drying Racks,

Once in residence on Brownsea, Charles and Florence van Raalte began to organise their household in the grand manner of upper-class Edwardian society. Naturally, the basis of this was a large servant population. The van Raaltes were, it would seem, good employers who treated their staff with respect and were certainly very different from the image of late nineteenth and early twentieth century estate owners that has become so familiar from television dramas. Soon after their arrival on Brownsea, Charles and Margherita covered themselves in old sacks and began painting gates, tarring railings and passing the time of day with the men and women who lived on the island. These were mainly farm-workers and gardeners who had been there since the Cavendish Bentinck and Balfour ownerships. Margherita's tasks included helping tune her father's many musical instruments and polishing the castle's suits of armour.

When the van Raaltes took on new staff, they were selected for their musical knowledge as much as their abilities as domestic servants or estate workers. Their secondary role would be as musicians in a proposed island band and by 1902 there was a nucleus for just such a grouping of musicians. Within a year of moving to Brownsea, the van Raaltes employed 71 people.

Horse and Carriage, Mr and Mrs van Raalte seated at the front

Below: Coachman George Chandler and five Strappers

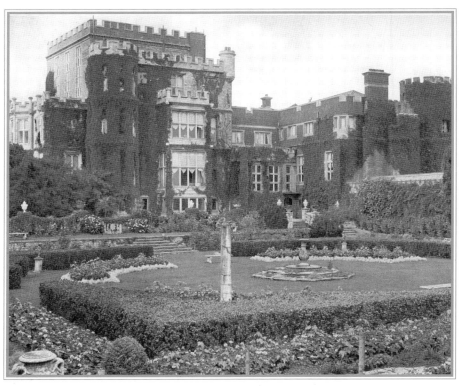

Castle Italian Garden

Their roles were as follows;

Steam yacht, 120 tons	9	Bricklayer's labourer	1
Steam yacht, 20 tons	3	Electrician	1
Launch boatman	1	Farm workers	7
Steward	1	Gardeners	10
Stables at Sandbanks	6	Gamekeepers	4
Servants at the castle	12	Estate workers	2
Laundry maids	2	Handyman	1
Carpenters	3	School teachers	2
Painters	3	Professional golfer	
Bricklayer	1		1

The laundry maids washed, dried and ironed the washing from the London residence as well as from the castle, using a building near the present public hide. The washing came in large wicker baskets by train from London. This seeming extravagance may well have been a sensible procedure because the water from the island's springs was almost certainly purer than London water and there was ample space for drying washing in the open air.

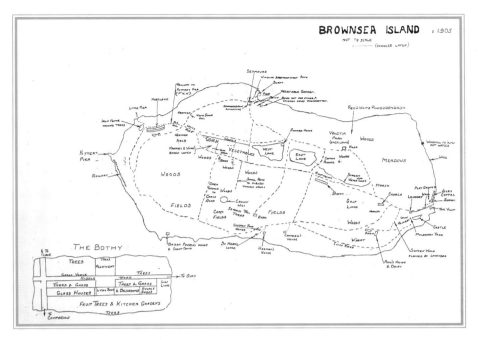

1905 Map

Mr van Raalte as Mayor of Poole
Mrs van Raalte

25

The castle's two very busy laundry maids would also have been paid less than their London counterparts.

Horses and carriages were bought and housed in the stables on the mainland at Sandbanks, and a new road to them from the main road (now Panorama Road) was built, and later handed over to Poole Corporation by Mr van Raalte. The stables included accommodation and were located on ground that is now part of the Royal Motor Yacht Club. Owning these mainland stables meant that Charles van Raalte had a property qualification within the jurisdiction of Poole Corporation.

After the local government reforms of 1894 Brownsea Island became part of the Studland Parish and among the first elected members of its council was a man called Alfred Barnard. According to the 1901 Census he was an "Estate Agent" living on Brownsea and his dedication to his new civic role is shown by the fact that he was one of only two members to turn up for the council's meeting in July 1900!

Charles van Raalte also took on a civic role and became Mayor of Poole in 1902, even though he was not an elected councillor. It was unusual, although not unknown, for prominent landowners to become Mayor of towns or cities within or adjoining their estates without having to go through the formality of an election. What was different about Poole and Mr van Raalte was that he had lived in the area for less than two years. He had clearly made an immediate impact on Poole's leading citizens. Having become Mayor of Poole, Charles van Raalte automatically became Admiral of the Port and, when he was in residence, was able to fly the Union Jack from the tower on the eastern side of the castle. Whenever a naval vessel passed the island, the flag was dipped in salute.

Charles van Raalte's benevolence towards his employees on the island is demonstrated by comparing their wages and conditions with those in Poole. The port and its related businesses had prospered during the eighteenth and early nineteenth centuries thanks to its deep involvement in the Newfoundland trade. Once this had ended, many families were living in great poverty, particularly those with homes on and around Poole Quay. It was common in this part of the town for several houses to share one privy. On Brownsea Island the average wage for a man was eighteen shillings a week plus free housing, whereas in Poole it was fifteen shillings and rent had to be paid from this amount. The Poole Herald reported that on Boxing Day 1902 Florence van Raalte invited 400 of Poole's poorest children to a seasonal tea at the Guildhall, which was suitably decorated for Christmas.

In June 1903 the van Raaltes, as Mayor and Mayoress, provided a tea party in Poole park for the town's school children, old people and the inmates of the workhouse. Eight hundred children, with their teachers or with Salvation Army officers for those not attending school, gathered at the park and began by marching past the Mayor, who was dressed in his robes. After the children had had their tea, a thousand adults then sat down to eat. There were bands playing, Punch and Judy shows, fairground rides and boat trips on the lakes. After five o'clock, the gates were opened to allow any resident entry and it was estimated that 16,000 people were present to watch the 'daylight' fireworks that rounded off the day.

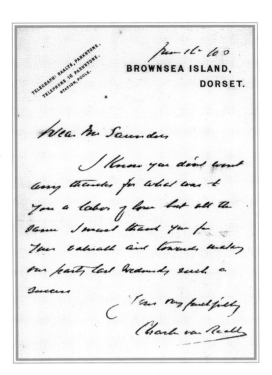

BROWNSEA ISLAND,
DORSET.

Two letters from Mr van Raalte

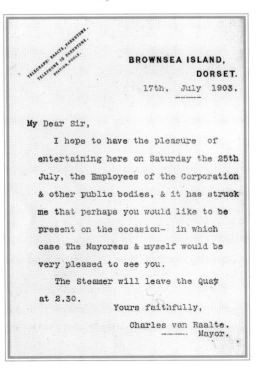

BROWNSEA ISLAND,
DORSET.

17th. July 1903.

My Dear Sir,

I hope to have the pleasure of entertaining here on Saturday the 25th July, the Employees of the Corporation & other public bodies, & it has struck me that perhaps you would like to be present on the occasion— in which case The Mayoress & myself would be very pleased to see you.

The Steamer will leave the Quay at 2.30.

Yours faithfully,

Charles van Raalte.
Mayor.

The following month, over 400 guests from among Poole Corporation's employees, along with their wives and girl friends, and men from the town's police force, fire brigade and those tramway employees who could be spared, were taken to Brownsea Island. With due consideration to the safety of the town, it had been arranged for police officers and firemen to be brought in from outside the borough. Although heavy rain curtailed the outside entertainment for those spending the day on Brownsea, they were invited into the castle where they heard music played on some of Mr van Raalte's wonderful collection of instruments. Because of the rain, tea was taken in small groups in a marquee rather than on open tables in the grounds. When the festivities ended, guests returned to Poole Quay on the steamship Telegraph which had to make several trips. As each boat load left the island, the departing guests gave three cheers for their hosts, Charles and Florence van Raalte.

Being the Mayor of Poole also meant that Charles van Raalte was a magistrate and a local newspaper, the Bournemouth Graphic, was fulsome in its praise for his open-handed generosity and his personal geniality. The article also listed his appearances and his support of school treats, at-homes, garden parties, fancy dress balls, sailing and rowing regattas and banquets! Christian Biggs remembered the regattas and the yachts with their different coloured sails and flags, and the crews in their striped stocking hats.

Charles was also a member of the Dorset Natural History and Antiquarian Field Club, the county's premier association for those interested in archaeology and natural history. Its membership largely consisted of the county's aristocracy and gentry, along with the man who is probably its most famous son, the novelist Thomas Hardy. The club visited Brownsea in 1905 for a talk by Charles van Raalte, a conducted tour of the grounds and a viewing of his splendid collection of musical instruments. So many members wished to attend this event that steam ship booked to carry them to the island had to tow a barge. Charles also sent his steam yacht and steam pinnace to assist in ferrying everyone from and to Poole.

MR. CHARLES VAN RAALTE,
(BROWNSEA ISLAND),
requests the favour of your support at the ensuing election.

MONOCHROME PUBLISHED BY THE BEX-HILL PRINTING CO., LTD., 10, BRIGHTON CHAMBERS, LONDON BRIDGE S.E.

Notice of Primrose League Meeting on Brownsea Island

He also established a large Reading Room on the island, for general use during the day and for the men to play billiards in the evening. It was also used as an indoor shooting range. Initially the Room was on the Quayside and later some say that it was in a hut built for the foresters in the First World War.

Like many other wealthy landowners, van Raalte was tempted to enter politics and his opportunity came in 1904 when the Member of Parliament for the East Dorset constituency, Humphrey Sturt, succeeded to the peerage and a seat in the Lords when his father, Lord Alington, died. Persuaded by Florence, Charles put his name forward and was adopted as the prospective Conservative and Unionist candidate.

In the run up to the by-election of 17 March 1904 there were a number of issues raised including education, free trade, reducing unemployment, better housing, Irish home rule, the poor working conditions of Chinese labourers in South African gold mines and temperance. This latter topic was probably raised because van Raalte, as Mayor, had chaired a meeting of the Church of England Temperance Society although he did not advocate total abstinence from alcohol, but only moderation.

His Liberal opponent, Charles Lyell, had made several uncomplimentary remarks about van Raalte in his adoption speech, saying that he had wobbled first on one and then on the other side of the fiscal fence, "with an ingenuity which would have earned him a fortune on the music hall stage." The public meetings at both the by-election and in the general election two years later were rowdy affairs. Margherita van Raalte remembered being in a coach pulled by four horses, waving a dark blue silk handkerchief from the windows, and being surprised when eggs and boards with protruding nails were thrown at them. Once, and only once, Margherita had to speak at an election gathering. She was dressed in black stockings, a short skirt and a high necked shirt, with her hair pulled back and a large black bow tied round a pigtail. There is no record of what she actually said! Charles van Raalte lost the seat to his Liberal opponent by 820 votes, but it says much for his efforts and popularity that in the 1906 general election he failed by only twenty one votes to take the seat. Given that this was the year of the great Liberal 'landslide', this was a remarkable achievement.

Beaters

Mrs van Raalte in the Castle Grounds

Guests & Visitors

Charles and Florence van Raalte were prominent members of London society and they attended many balls and parties when in the capital. Brownsea was, in effect, their country estate and its castle was their manor house. When in residence on the island they were able to offer their visitors a variety of leisure pursuits such as sailing, shooting, playing tennis, and the use of a nine hole golf course, as well as dancing and fine dining at their banquets. Charles wrote a history of the island which Florence illustrated and copies of this were given to their visitors. It was published by the London firm of Arthur L. Humphreys in 1906 and the bookplate incorporated the da Costa family crest, presumably as a gesture to Charles' mother.

All these activities meant that the islanders could enjoy a more varied employment than had existed before the coming of the van Raaltes to Brownsea. As well as the normal duties associated with the running of a wealthy man's country home, such as preparing food and waiting at table, there was caddying for the golfers and beating for the shooters. Charles van Raalte even employed a golf professional named Charlie Major.

Visitors came from all over Europe, usually arriving in Poole by train from London and then travelling to the island from Poole Quay aboard Charles' 25 ton yacht *Blunderbuss*. As mentioned earlier, until the end of the 19th Century the island was known as Branksea or Branksea Island. It seems that both "Brownsea" and "Branksea" were used by the inhabitants of Poole and the islanders themselves. Curiously, in 1899, a sales notice is entitled "Branksea" but another document, from 1892, has "Brownsea." It was Florence van Raalte who settled the matter once and for all for she became aware that many of the castle's guests were leaving the train two stops early, at Branksome Station, rather than Poole. To a stranger, Branksome and Branksea were obviously confusing, so she decreed that the island would henceforth be known only as Brownsea.

Florence was very conscious of the social manners of the era and was keen that her children should show the proper respect to her royal guests. If she wanted the children to bow or curtsy in the presence of royalty, she would signal this by pretending to brush a fly or wasp from her face. This gesture was copied many years later by Margherita when, with her own children, she visited Brownsea Island. Margherita's only son, John, would refer to his grandmother as "Mrs van Royalty" because of her large number of foreign acquaintances. On one occasion she was delighted to have 28 visitors with royal titles sitting down to lunch.

Signed Photograph from the Queen of Romania

Just one year separated Noel and Margherita but there was a third child, Gwendoline, who was about three years younger. She was called "Babs" by her brother and sister until they were all present at a lunch attended by Olga Montagu, aunt of the then Lord Montagu of Beaulieu. As the youngest child she was always trying to attract attention and often did not conform to the expected rules of behaviour. At the lunch Gwendoline interrupted the adults' conversation with a saucy remark and Olga Montagu glared at her and said "Poots to you." From that day onwards Gwendoline was called "Poots" by the family.

House Party Group

BROWNSEA CASTLE. Date_____		Post Arrives 8 a.m. 3 p.m.	Leaves 9.30 a.m. 4.30 p.m.
BEDROOMS.	VISITORS.		
Periwinkle		Sunday	
Jasmine		Arrives 8 a.m. Leaves 10 a.m.	
Ivy		Boat leaves	For Trains leave Poole / Arriving London
Lavender		7.45	8.44 — 11.0
Rosemary		10	10.57 — 2
Shamrock		12.30	1.38 — 4.0
Thistle			3.36 — 6.45
Moss Rose		6.46	6.46 — 10.5
Hydrangea			Sunday — Sunday
Daphne			5.32 — 8.13
Hollyhock			6.18 — 9.5
Myrtle			
Cowslip		VISITING SERVANTS. Maids.	
Pansy			
Red Clover	TOWER.		
Daisy			
Violet			
Cornflower		VALETS ROOMS.	
Buttercup			
Fuschia			
Carnation			
Poppy			
Daffodil			

Names of Rooms with Postal and Train Times

Members of royal families from all over Europe were regular guests of the van Raaltes with probably the most colourful, in both dress and character, being Queen Marie, wife of King Ferdinand of Romania. She looked like a fairytale queen, dressed in flowing gowns and bedecked in jewellery and crowned with a pearl tiara. Her theatrical persona was enhanced by her habit of handing out signed photographs of herself. Her sister was Princess Beatrice, wife to the Spanish Prince Alfonso Marie of Orleans, and his mother was among the visitors to Brownsea. Beatrice and Alfonso's sons Prince Alphonso and Prince Luis, although older than the van Raalte children, were great friends of Noel and Margherita from their time in Brighton. The list of royal visitors seems endless and included many members of the Bourbon and Battenberg families, along with Prince George (later the Duke of Kent) and Edward, Prince of Wales (later Edward VII).

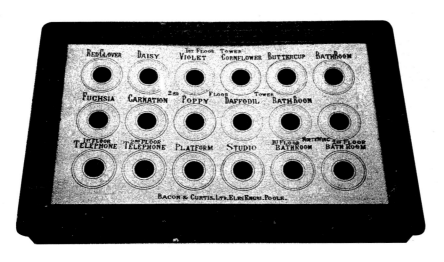

Servants' Bells

33

Many of their guests brought a manservant or lady's maid with them and so that all of the visitors and their staff could find their rooms Mrs van Raalte named each bedroom after flowers. Each guest and servant was given a card telling which room was theirs. Other essential information was included on the card including times of the mail collection and the times of trains from Poole to London. For the castle servants, there was a direct benefit from the presence of some many wealthy guests in the forms of tips. These were usually very generous, with the King and Queen of Romania giving £5 each, and the "top man" on the staff receiving £10.

One notable visitor in these early years was the hero of the Siege of Mafeking during the Boer War. This was Lieutenant General (later Lord) Baden-Powell, whom the van Raaltes had met whilst they were on holiday in Ireland, and who already had some knowledge of Brownsea because he, as a young man, had landed there without permission. Now, as an invited guest, he sketched, painted in watercolours and invented songs. He was keen to develop outdoor pursuits for young people and he tried out his ideas on Margherita and Nony: they were later to regard themselves as the first Boy Scouts! Robert Baden-Powell was given permission by the van Raaltes to hold a camp on the island with twenty neighbours' sons and another twenty boys from the "roughest part of Poole." However, records show that the 20 boys who came to the camp were mostly from the Boys' Brigade or from Private or Public schools and were certainly none of the "mischievous boys hanging around Poole Quay!"

Baden-Powell Experimental Scout Camp. Inset: Baden-Powell c1909

This first camp, which was held from 1 August until the morning of 9 August 1907, was to ensure Brownsea Island's place in history and is described in detail in Brian Woolgar and Sheila La Riviere's *Why Brownsea? Beginning of Scouting*. From this initial camp came the formation of the Boy Scout Movement and the emergence of a world-wide organisation.

One night, during the camp, Nony and Margherita crept up to one of the tents where the boys were sleeping. However, as the camp had been organised on military lines, there was a cry of, "Who goes there?" They were led to Baden-Powell's tent for a severe telling-off, although they detected a wink from the great man. Interestingly, some of the island's inhabitants were not aware of the experimental camp. One, young Daisy Toms, did meet some of the boys and took them home to her mother who gave them some home-made cakes!

Another notable visitor was Guglielmo Marconi (1847-1937) who had been given a room and a workshop in the Haven Hotel, at the entrance to the harbour, in order to further his experiments in wireless telegraphy. Nony and Margherita used to row across to the Haven and watch him at work and were fascinated by his discoveries. On one occasion they saw Marconi's chief engineer using curved copper plates at each end of the room and it was explained that this brought in more wavelengths, thus preventing the sound overlapping in the air.

One Christmas Marconi gave Nony and Margherita a small wooden box each, measuring about one foot square by six inches and with a aerial four feet high. On top was a "tickety tick" apparatus – the lever used for tapping out Morse code. Eventually Tommy (later Lord Howard de Walden and Margherita's husband) helped them set up the apparatus in Margherita's bedroom in the castle tower and in Nony's workshop in the Villina (now the Villano and the National Trust coffee shop). They were thus able to "morse" *(A is .-, N is -., P is .-. etc)* messages to each other. This skill was extremely useful to the two children for at dinner, where they were expected to be seen but not heard, they would send messages to each other across the table by blinking. A left eye blink was dot and a right eye blink was dash. Guests would wonder why the children were smiling when nothing amusing had been said! Marconi explained his experiments to the children and prophesied to Margherita that in the future people would be able to "see through walls", speak in words across the world instead of having use Morse, have music relayed into their homes and communicate over distances whilst walking about. He was absolutely right! It has been said that Marconi was given rooms at the Haven Hotel because he did not have the money to finance his experiments. However, he did have an enormous yacht, the Elettra, and it was on this vessel that he entertained the van Raaltes to dinner. After the meal they listened to a boxing match relayed from New York and were amazed that the sound could cross the Atlantic to Poole harbour in a fraction of a second!

Like most ladies in high society, Florence van Raalte saw herself as a match-maker and one of her more unusual schemes involved Marconi. The other party was the Hon. Beatrice O'Brien, daughter of the 14th Baron Inchiquin and a member of one of Ireland's oldest aristocratic families, and she with her mother had been visiting Lady Howard de

Walden at Chirk Castle when she received an invitation from Mrs van Raalte to stay at the newly purchased Brownsea Castle. It was unusual, of course, for young society ladies to stay away from home without a parent or at a house with people unknown to their circle of friends, but Beatrice was nevertheless allowed to visit Brownsea. When she arrived at the castle there was a lot of talk about Marconi and what he was doing in the area. Beatrice had heard of Guglielmo Marconi and knew that he and Lord Howard de Walden were among the first owners of Mercedes cars in England. She also knew that both men were older than herself. She was even more surprised when Marconi was due to visit Brownsea Island, and Mrs van Raalte suggested that Beatrice go to the Castle Pier to meet him. Marconi was immediately bedazzled by her looks and conversation, and became a frequent visitor to the island, neglecting his scientific experiments. Marconi was, in fact, already engaged to be married to an American, Miss Inez Milholland, but he asked her to release him from this commitment.

Marconi managed to get permission from Mrs van Raalte to drive Beatrice to London but she was conscious of society conventions and declined his offer, travelling instead by train with her maid. Later, Marconi bought a ticket for a charity ball at the Albert hall organised by Lady Inchiquin, Beatrice's widowed mother. He found Beatrice at the top of the long iron stairs of the outer lobby and, in this unromantic spot, proposed marriage. Beatrice was proud to be asked for her hand by such a famous person but he was very unlike the beaux of her own age. She had not expected the proposal and, afraid of her mother's response, for she was hoping that her daughter would marry a rich and titled man, Beatrice asked for time to think. As the days passed, Marconi deluged her with letters. Eventually he was invited to tea but, to his surprise, Beatrice declined his marriage proposal.

Marconi was terribly upset by this rejection. He did not return to his experiments and instead visited eastern Europe where he planned the setting up of new telegraph communication stations. It was at this time that he contracted malaria and the fevers from this illness were to plague him for many years.

The following summer Beatrice was again invited to Brownsea Island and Mrs van Raalte had promised her that Marconi would not be there. However, Florence was intent on the match and invited Marconi to return from his foreign travels to Brownsea. Beatrice was soon to be seen walking or sailing with Marconi and he again asked her to marry him. On this occasion she agreed, providing that her sister Lilah approved. She also met with her brother Barney who was visiting Brownsea and whilst he was delighted at the news, said that she must inform her mother and gain her approval, along with that of the head of the family, her eldest brother Lucius, the 15th Lord Inchiquin.

Marconi and Beatrice duly went to London to inform the two senior members of the family, having just bought her 'tremendous' engagement ring. When Marconi asked Lady Inchiquin for her daughter's hand in marriage, she was not encouraging and said that Lucius should have the final say. However Lady Inchiquin managed to speak to her son before Marconi and Beatrice reached him and they were told to break off the engagement. Beatrice refused, but was upset when a newspaper gossip column implied that Marconi, whilst on a trip to Rome, had "kept company" with an Italian princess and had even shared a box at the opera with her! A strong minded old aunt, Lady Metcalfe, who was consulted in times of crisis, could not understand how Beatrice had allowed herself to become engaged to a 'foreigner'. She was unaware that Marconi was half Irish, for his mother was from County Wexford.

When Marconi heard of the gossip about his "engagement" to an Italian princess, he returned to London. Beatrice's family were impressed by the speed of his return and were seduced by his charm and elegance. They felt that he was, above all, a "gentleman" and an international figure who was becoming more and more acceptable to "Society." They duly blessed the engagement and it was announced in the Court Circular. He married her on 16 March 1905, presumably to the great satisfaction of Florence van Raalte.

The Haven Hotel, 1898. Marconi established here a wireless station in October for his early transmissions. He kept it for experimental work until 1926.

The Brownsea Island Estate Band

A particular feature of the van Raaltes' time on Brownsea was Charles' creation of the island's 'Estate Band' or, to give it its proper title, The Brownsea Island Estate Brass and Reed Band. Given Charles' love of music and his huge collection of instruments, this was probably an inevitable innovation. It was certainly one that gave Charles and Florence a great deal of pleasure during their years on Brownsea.

All of the musicians were part of the estate's workforce, and there were originally 22 of them, rising to a maximum of 27. Each member wore a blue uniform with a cap, and there were red cuffs on the jacket and a red stripe down each trouser leg. The bandmaster's uniform had silver fittings and a white bandolier. Everything, uniforms and instruments, mainly flutes, cornets, piccolos and trombones, were paid for by Charles van Raalte.

The bandmaster was Alfred Campbell, previously a foreman with the building firm Rigler, with eighteen men working under him. He had worked on the restoration of the castle after the fire of 1896 and had been recommended to Charles van Raalte by Major Balfour as being an excellent carpenter. Until Rose Cottage, near the southern shore, was renovated, Mr Campbell and his family lived in the Villa. The 1901 Census shows him to be 38 years old and his occupation is given as Head Estate Carpenter. He is recorded as living with his wife Mary, aged 40, his daughter Louise (known as Lou) aged eleven, and his mother, Hannah, aged 76 and a retired laundress. Louise Campbell (later Brayley) speaking in 1966 remembered that the Villa had five rooms and that the sitting room had a beautiful bay window. The census also reveals that there was a maid, implying that she also 'lived in' at the much smaller Rose Cottage, which had just two bedrooms, after the family moved from the Villa. A coalhouse and a washhouse with a 'copper' in it were built on to Rose Cottage.

Alfred Campbell was still living at the Villa when Charles van Raalte formed the Island Band and it was there that they held their weekly rehearsals. When the Campbells moved to Rose Cottage some of the band's rehearsals were held there, even though it was so cramped that Mary Campbell had to pin the music on the walls. The band had a varied and extensive repertoire and performed frequently on the island in places such as around the flagpole on the Quay, which had grass around it then, at the castle as guests went into dinner, at the balls held in the castle, on the lawns, and at most of the gatherings held in the castle gardens. William Dean noted that the band played before 800 people when the Primrose League* held a meeting there.

* The Primrose League was a Conservative Association organisation formed in memory of Benjamin Disraeli whose favorite button hole was a Primrose.

On the mainland they played at van Raalte's election meetings, at fêtes and Primrose League fund raising events. Playing on the mainland was considered an 'immense treat.' A Royal Blue charabanc with tiered seating and a canvas sliding hood transported them, and concerts were given as far away as Shaftesbury and Lyme Regis, as well as in Poole.

On one occasion the band played at the Elms Estate in Parkstone, with a second performance on the green outside the coastguard cottages at Sandbanks. At the appointed time for this later performance, only two bandsmen appeared. The remainder had been drinking at the bar of the (old) Haven Hotel and when they left, dressed of course in their full uniforms, they were in no fit state to play. They fell 'like ninepins' in Banks Road, damaging their instruments. There is no record of Charles van Raalte hearing about this episode so perhaps it was hushed up!

Estate Band - 1. Mr. Goddard, 2. Tom Webb, 3. Fred Dean, 4. Charlie Watson, 5. Stanley Northover, 6. Mr. Cobb, 7. Billy Dean, 8. Mr. Norwood, 9. Alf Dean, 10. Alf Toms, 11. Frank Noble, 12. Mr. Chilkit, 13. Mr. McLean, 14. Mr. Dobell, 15, Andrew Halliday, 16. Mr. Tresco-Brown, 17. Mr. Campbell, 18. Mr. G. Brown, 19. Mr. Northover, 20. Edward Aldridge, 21. Mr. F. B. Brattrick, 22. Chris Biggs.

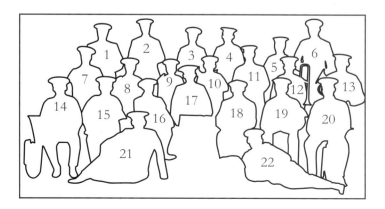

A
Sacred ♥ Concert

BY THE

Brownsea Island Estate Brass & Reed Band,

SUNDAY, AUGUST 27th, 1905,

Commencing at 5-30

PROGRAMME.

1.—Slow March—From Scipio	*Handel.*
2.—Anthem—" How beautiful upon the mountains "	*R. A. Smith.*
3.—Carol—" Sing to the Lord "	*Jackson.*
4.—Anthem—" To Thee O Lord "	*Leach.*
5.—Chorus—" Diadem "	*Anon.*
6.—Anthem—" The Earth is the Lords "	*R. A. Smith.*
7.—Carol—" With Cheerful notes "	*Dr. Taylor.*
8.—Anthem—" Jerusalem, my Glorious Home "	*L. Mason.*
9.—Chorus—" Blow ye the Trumpet, blow "	*Handel.*
10.—Anthem—" Save me O God "	*Round.*
11.—Anthem—" I will arise "	*Cecil.*
12.—Hymn—" Sun of my soul "	*Anon.*

GOD SAVE THE KING.

Conductor :—MR. A. E. CAMPBELL.

Band Programmes

Part I

Play. — The Lacemaker

Lacemaker.
- Lola — L. Campbell
- Clotilde — K. Backwell
- Benita — B. Harman
- Teresa — D. Lemon
- Juana — A. Biggs

Fairy Queen — F. Battrick
Fairies — M. Battrick - G. Toms. A. Phillips - V. Chandler
Dewdrops. G. Battrick - M. Biggs. D. Harman. J. Battrick. K. Battrick - B. Battrick

2 — Sailor's Song
3 — Sailor's Hornpipe
4 — Dad's Allotment. E. Norwood
5 — Pirouette Dance
6 — Song. Watching for Dad. G. Toms - E. Battrick. J. Battrick
7 — Flag Drill
8 — Bridesmaids' Dance

Part II

1 — Cantata. The Fairies' Visit
2 — Pixies' Dance
3 — Dorothy Noll. E. Battrick
4 — Duet. D. Harman - E. Norwood
5 — Louisiana Dance
6 — Big Steamers. G. Toms. M. Battrick - A. Phillips. E. Battrick - D. Harman. E. Norwood
7 — Professor Tomkins' Talking Figures
8 — Irish Jig
9 — Khaki Song
10 — Mazurka

March.—"Rocked in the Cradle of the Deep."	Selection.—"National Melodies." .. *R. De Lacy.*
H. Round.	Polka.—"The Queen's Visit." .. *H. Round.*
Valse.—"The Little Flirt." .. *T. H. Wright.*	March.—"Lancaster.".. .. *H. Round.*
Slow March.—"The March of the Men of Montgomery-shire." .. *J. Ord Hume.*	Valse.—"The Bonnie Princess." .. *R. De Lacy.*
Cornet Solo.—"Killarney." . *Balf.* Mr. W. Willis.	Schottische.—"The Heather Queen." *W. T. Harris.*
March.—"Maid of Athens." .. *H. R. Allen.*	Polka.--"Fancy Free." *W. T. Harris.*
Valse.—"Sunflower." .. .. *H. Round.*	March.—"Fearless." .. .. *J. Moss.*
Selection.—"Gems of Scotland." .. *R. De Lacy.*	Valse.—"Sweet Lorna." *R. De Lacy.*
Glee.—"Here's a Health to all good Lasses."	Polka.—"Daisy Dell.".. . *R. De Lacy.*
March.—"York." .. .. *H. Round.*	Song.—"Home Sweet Home." ..

Conductor:—Mr. A. E. Campbell. **God save the King.**

41

Islanders *

The population of Brownsea can be divided into two categories, those who lived in and around the castle and those who lived at Maryland on the western side of the island. This latter community was made up of the estate workers and consisted of twenty houses in five blocks of four, built fifty years earlier by Colonel Waugh as part of his grand scheme to capitalise on the islands china clay. Each house had just two bedrooms, so Charles van Raalte, in a typical act of generosity, allowed those with large families to combine two houses, thus giving each four bedrooms. The first two families to benefit from this were the Hydes and the Toms. Downstairs there was a dining room, sitting room and a kitchen, along with a washhouse and a storeroom which was mainly used for wood and coal. This room was later used as a dance room even though it still contained the built in 'copper' for boiling clothes or Christmas puddings! They had pretty gardens in the front, facing the 'coach road' which ran round the island, parallel to the shore. The views across to Poole or Wareham were marvellous, albeit rather spoilt by the rubbish dumped by the side of the path to the shore.

Fred Toms, a bricklayer, and his wife Alice (née Frampton) moved to Brownsea from Highcliffe in 1902 and Daisy, their fifth child of eleven, wrote her story for her son Melvin Chapman (known as 'Chappie') in 1976 when she was 83 years old. Alice Toms, with baby Alfred (the ninth child, born in April 1901) went by train to Poole while the furniture and the rest of the family travelled in a horse drawn van. The furniture then went by the 'horse boat' barge whilst the family were taken by the island ferry *Blunderbuss* to Maryland. Mrs Hyde, wife of the island's painter and another Maryland resident, welcomed them with tea and cakes and the family soon became an established part of the community.

The Toms had a house in the centre of a terrace. Water for all the Maryland cottages was obtained from one large pump situated behind their house. The stone yard at the back of the house, flanked by the kitchen and washhouse, faced south and was a sun trap. There was a long garden above the yard reached by a winding path. Each garden had a brick built lavatory and inside there was a seat with a hole in it. Underneath was a bucket, which when full was lugged up the back garden, and dumped in the wider section at the end. This would certainly have contributed to the high yields of vegetables in that area! Fruit bushes and vegetables were grown, in the garden, washing dried, chickens had a coop there and, later, there was even a pig. The chickens were kept for their eggs but occasionally one would be used for a weekend lunch.

* see Appendix C for details of some of the families on the island.

Mr and Mrs Saville at the front of their house at Maryland

Back of Savilles' House

The areas of heather on the island attracted huge numbers of bees. Fred Toms kept bees in 'little white houses' at the top of the garden, although in winter they were taken into an empty house. He was frequently stung but this did not bother him as he thought bee stings prevented rheumatism in later life. This proved not to be true as he did indeed suffer from rheumatism as he got older! The honey from the bees was stored in a galvanised bath. So much was produced that everyone in Maryland was given a jar and Alice Toms used it to make mead. Elderberry and parsnip wines were also made, together with a 'wonderful tonic for the blood', wood sage tea. It was extremely bitter, despite looking like strong tea.

Coal was the basic fuel for heating houses and was brought to Brownsea, in the early days, by square-rigged sailing ship with 200 tons being delivered at a time to the island's quayside, a mile and a half from Maryland. Hundredweight sacks were taken to the coal store, now the National Trust reception room, and from there it was delivered by horse and cart to each house. Later, coal was brought across from Poole using the horse-boat.

Another islander, Freeland Battrick, started work there in 1887 and at first he travelled daily from Studland. After 1890 he lodged at Maryland with a Mr and Mrs Whittingham. He met his future wife, Hannah Hooper, at the Haven Hotel where she worked and they were married in 1903. They took up residence in one of the farm cottages, eventually moving to a cottage on the Quay. They had eight children, and one

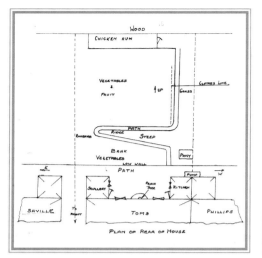

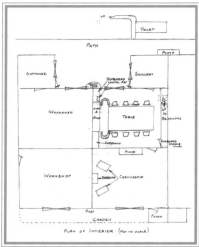

Sketches of the Toms' House (two combined) at Maryland
Sketch of the Toms' back Garden

Daisy Toms in front of
Landing Prohibited notice

son, Jack, and six girls survived. Freeland and Hannah admired the caring nature and benevolence of Mr and Mrs van Raalte and named their first child Florence. Their youngest daughter, Dorothy, had the distinction of being the last child to attend the island school and she was its only pupil when the authorities closed it in 1928.

Although the islanders were almost self-sufficient for food, shopping in Poole was popular. Tom Dean ran a ferry service to Poole from the island quay and on Saturday, some of the Maryland residents, including the Toms and the Hydes, used it. They would push a handcart to the quay and, on return, would load it up with all that they had bought in Poole and push it the mile and a half to Maryland. However, friends and relatives visiting the islanders could only land if they had permission from Mr van Raalte or his Steward (sometimes referred to as the Estate Agent.). They would normally travel in one of Harveys' launches from Sandbanks, or with a water-postman from Poole.

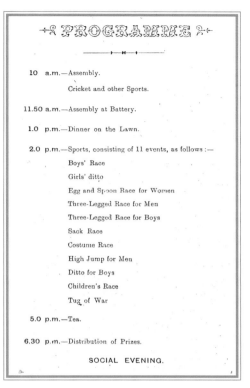

❧ PROGRAMME ❧

10 a.m.—Assembly.

        Cricket and other Sports.

11.50 a.m.—Assembly at Battery.

1.0 p.m.—Dinner on the Lawn.

2.0 p.m.—Sports, consisting of 11 events, as follows :—

        Boys' Race

        Girls' ditto

        Egg and Spoon Race for Women

        Three-Legged Race for Men

        Three-Legged Race for Boys

        Sack Race

        Costume Race

        High Jump for Men

        Ditto for Boys

        Children's Race

        Tug of War

5.0 p.m.—Tea.

6.30 p.m.—Distribution of Prizes.

        SOCIAL EVENING.

Sports Day programme.
Below: Tea Party at the Castle, Mrs van Raalte and
Tresco Brown on the left

It was not always necessary for people to cross the island to the quay when they wanted to go to Poole because on the Maryland shoreline was the 'Little Pier.' Dinghies were tied to it and, when the tide was in, they could row across to the town. If they planned on going to Poole when the tide was out, the boat was taken in advance to the deeper water at Pottery Pier. It was usual for Mr and Mrs Toms and Mr and Mrs Hyde to go together by dinghy to Poole on Saturday evening. Mrs Toms' brother Frank Frampton had a butcher's shop at Highcliffe and he and his wife would sometimes meet the two couples from Brownsea, bringing 'delicious faggots' for them. They would meet at Gambier's* on Poole Quay, where the three ladies would have to sit in the back parlour as only men were allowed to drink in the bar.

* *Gambier's is the King's Head public House, at No. 6 High Street. Edward Evan Gambier was the publican from 1911 to 1913*

The weather could be a problem for people crossing to Poole and on one Saturday night, the Toms and the Hydes became lost in thick fog on their way home. Rather than drifting aimlessly they dropped anchor. When the fog lifted at daybreak, they found that they were only a few yards from Little Pier and could have walked ashore at Maryland. Alf Toms had learned how to play the cornet, and when he knew that islanders would be returning to Maryland through the fog, he would go down to the shore and play his cornet, but although it could be heard, those who were fog-bound could not be certain of the direction of the sound.

A highlight of island life was travelling by paddle steamer to Bournemouth. Tom Pool, the Head Gardener, would take his children and their young friends in a small boat out into mid-stream, near the Bell Buoy where the paddle-steamer Lord Elgin would slow down and they would climb onto the paddle box to get aboard. 'Just like getting on a bus', said daughter Amy. In 1901 Tom was taking two of his sons Fred and Leonard to Parkstone Pier in a small dinghy when a strong wind blew up and they were in danger of capsizing. He told the boys to pray and say 'Jesus said, Peace Be Still.' This they did and they reached Parkstone Pier safely.

Tom Pool's family consisted of his second wife, Rose, and their six children and they lived for seven years in a cottage near the farm at the island's eastern end. Each day he would pick a posy (called 'malmaison' by his family) of parma violets for Florence van Raalte which she would tuck into her waistband. Being Head Gardener could be a seven day a week job, for he would even check the greenhouses on a Sunday. In notes made in later years by his youngest daughter Dorothy and her sister Amy, they remembered that the greenhouses had clusters of black grapes, along with peaches and nectarines. There were nets strung below to catch the fruit and the sisters also remembered that a chameleon lived in one of the greenhouses.

The farm cottages also housed other families, such as the Broomfields and the Strongs who kept pigs, ducks, geese and chickens. At one stage, the Broomfield family lived at the Bothy, built on the north side of the Vinery wall. The Bothy's usual purpose was to house two or three single men whose jobs included keeping the fires going to heat the water for the greenhouse pipes. The gardeners living in the Bothy were looked after by a maid and it was quite common for the young woman performing this role to marry one of them, thus qualifying for a house on the island. The Fisher family lived at Maryland but when Mr Fisher became butler to Mr van Raalte they moved to a house near the clock tower.

The island's Home Farm was an integral part of Brownsea's economy and had twelve milking cows, six heifers, one bull, six sows, one boar, four cart-horses, three riding ponies and 64 sheep. There were also chickens, turkeys, geese, ducks and guinea fowl. Food was put out for the wild creatures such as pigeons, doves and peacocks whilst, every year, four or five thousand pheasants were bred for the van Raaltes' shooting parties. As well as the common pheasants, there were also Mongolian, Chinese, Gold and Silver ones. Five hundred rainbow trout were introduced into the top (West) lake. One problem was deer which did a lot of damage to the crops of wheat, barley, spring and winter oats, swedes, turnips, cabbage and maize. The rat population was kept down by putting a bounty on them – their tails were worth a penny each to the islanders.

The estate cows were given names such as Buttercup, Maud, Alice, Polly, Tulip, May and Curly, according to the surviving metal nameplates which hung from their stalls in the cowshed. Between the cowshed and the farm cottages was a large wooden building, now demolished, which housed horses and cattle, along with wagons. It also acted as a hay store. The cows grazed in the field facing the farm, now Church Field, which was fenced and was entered by an iron gate near the church, and also in water meadows which now form the Lagoon. Brownsea was self sufficient in eggs, butter, milk and cheese, whilst vegetables and cereals were grown as well, mainly on the southern side of the island.

The Campbells kept sheep in the field above Rose Cottage and, further west, the Harmans kept poultry. The brick-built poultry feed hut still stands but lacks its chimney. This building is often open at weekends as an information point, and contains the copper which was used to boil the scraps for feeding the poultry. In the fields facing Clown Hill peas, beetroot, potatoes, wheat and oats were grown. In summer the farm workers' day began at six in the morning, returning home for breakfast at eight. In winter they finished work at 4 pm. Without exception, every account of life on Brownsea Island describes the van Raaltes as good, caring employers and says it was happy place in which to live and work.

Harvesting oats

Island Children

Brownsea was an idyllic place for children, who made their own fun and games as, of course, did village children on the mainland. Hide-and-seek and tree climbing were popular and one girl, Nellie Hyde, seemed to attract trouble. On one occasion she lost her shoe in a cornfield and on another, she slipped when climbing a tree and was caught upside down by her knickers. During most winters, the two lakes (now part of the Dorset Wildlife Trust's reserve) would be covered with ice. Daisy Toms' eldest brother George, a gardener in the gardens near the greenhouse, would tie a rope round his waist for the youngsters to hold while he skated.

Daisy, daughter of Fred and Alice Toms*, and Gwen van Raalte, known as Miss Gwen to the islanders, were about the same age and despite the differences in their social status, became very friendly when they were about eleven years old. Thanks to Gwen, Daisy was introduced to upper class activities such as pony riding, tennis, croquet and clock golf. They also managed to get up to all sorts of mischief together. On one occasion they decided to taste some beetroot growing in a field – raw of course – using a piece of wire mesh fence to scrape off the mud and skin. After a few bites their mouths were purple and despite using water from the lake, they could not wash the colour off. They finally went into the castle grounds by a side entrance and the cook pulled them in through a kitchen window and managed to clean them up. She did not tell their parents.

Daisy Toms on the Church Roof

More conventional food was to be found in the fruit gardens or greenhouses and as long as Miss Gwen was present, they were not stopped from helping themselves. One afternoon, when in the castle grounds, a servant brought them the thinnest bread and butter sandwiches that Daisy had ever seen. When she went home, she told her mother that she was still starving. Both girls enjoyed

* *References to the Toms family are from the unpublished 'Brownsea Toms' by Chappie (Melvin) Chapman.*

Footprints carved on the Church roof

Mrs Toms' freshly baked cakes and bread and would call in to sample them whenever they caught the smell of them.

Dorothy Carr (née Pool) the daughter of Head Gardener Tom Pool, lived in one of the farm cottages on the edge of the Church field. She remembered the church tower as being a 'temptation' and that her two brothers, Leonard and Albert, had climbed to the top via the outside wall! Another temptation was to climb the inside stairs to the top of the tower and mark their footprint on the lead roof. They did this with the edge of the tower door key and then engraved their name inside the footprint. When Dorothy and her two brothers were doing this, the key broke and by coincidence the door slammed shut and the broken key would not open it, so they were trapped at the top of the church tower. Nobody passed by, and it was becoming dark when they managed to attract the attention of a dairyman as he walked by. He told their father, who knew of a spare key and released them. Research by National Trust volunteer Alan Marsh has identified several of the footprints including E Broomfield 1907, L R Pool, Lily Toms, Daisy Toms, Dorothy Holloway, David Holloway 25.6.1924, and the name Saville.

Dorothy was also able to ride Miss Gwen's Shetland pony. Miss Gwen would 'whack its backside' so that the pony would gallop away carrying Dorothy. Miss Gwen was also a fairly accomplished rider of some of the island's cattle but Dorothy could not be persuaded to emulate her!

Dorothy Toms remembered that when she lived at Highcliffe the big event of the week was having a penny to spend on sweets but, when the family moved to Brownsea, she found many more interesting and enjoyable things to do than eating sweets. Adults and children were expert rowers and most were strong swimmers. Several rowing boats were kept on the shore for the islanders to use if they wanted to go fishing or go across to Poole. As well as swimming when the tide was in, and paddling when it was out, she could pick winkles and cockles. The children learned to spot where cockles could be found by a small black patch in the mud, or by seeing 'two shining eyes.' Once gathered, the cockles were soaked in salted water and cooked the next day. Cockle picking was not without its dangers, though, for on one occasion Vi Toms became stuck in the mud up to her ankles and Daisy, when she tried to help, also became stuck. Fortunately Mr van Raalte was out walking and held out his walking stick for them to catch hold of, and pulled them out. They noticed that his white shoes had become plastered with mud.

Noel van Raalte, or Nony as he was known in the family, was very keen on engineering and in the Villano (referred to as Villina in Pages from my Life) he had a workshop with two lathes, an electric drill and workbenches. Whilst at Eton he built an Indian canoe for himself and his two sisters to sail on the harbour. He was a good swimmer and was awarded a testimonial, printed on vellum, from the Royal Humane Society for 'rescuing T R Pool from the harbour in August 1904'.

Miss Gwen was not welcomed into Noel's workshop as she touched things and chattered too much! However, Margherita was allowed to take the motorcycle engine to pieces, clean and oil the parts and then Noel would reassemble them. Noel's ambitions did not fit those of a son from a typical well off Edwardian family. He was usually covered in grease, wore dungarees (overalls), always had his sleeves rolled up and was often late for meals. His mother had hoped that he would become an officer in a Guards regiment but he was not tall enough. He disappointed his father by his lack of interest in music although he apparently knew most of the tunes and lyrics of Gilbert and Sullivan's comic operas.

Singing and music making were popular pastimes in many Victorian and Edwardian homes and Mr van Raalte had, of course, a passion for music. Most of the men interviewed for work on Brownsea were chosen mainly because of their musical ability so singing and music making featured strongly in their homes.

The Pool family were no exception and on Sunday evenings they sang hymns with Mrs Pool playing the piano whilst her husband and the five children all sang lustily. After the hymns came the Bible reading with Dorothy, the youngest child, sitting on her father's knee whilst he read stories and showed them pictures from a large and beautifully coloured Bible. Saturday night was bath night, using a tub in front of a huge fire and sometimes Miss Gwen would come in and help bath the younger children. Indeed, all three van Raalte children were frequent visitors to the Pool house which was near the Castle in a cottage close to the farm buildings.

Daisy Toms remembered the games the children played at home in the winter. They would walk on chairs until they reached the one behind their father, when he would pull them over his head, passing them on to their mother who was sitting opposite her husband. At meal times the children could only talk to their parents, not to their brothers and sisters. On one occasion Charles made his sister Daisy laugh by pulling faces at her and she was ordered by her mother to leave the table if she could not behave. Unfortunately Charles' serious expression made Daisy giggle again and she did indeed have to leave the table. Afterwards, though, Charles brought her a piece of cake.

Grace was said before each meal and they ate all that was put before them. Prayers were said before going to bed. On Saturday morning the children had a number of jobs to do such as cleaning shoes, polishing knives, forks and brass doorknobs 'ready for Sunday.' They all went to Sunday School which was held during the morning at a house in Maryland. Amy Pool gave Vi and Daisy Toms and Nellie Hyde piano lessons once a week. Mr Toms had a good baritone voice and was also a fine violinist. His sons all learned to play several musical instruments.

In the 1950s, a time when Brownsea was owned by Mrs Bonham Christie and normally closed to visitors, Amy Stace (née Pool) did manage to visit the island. The dereliction of the houses, farm and church were, for her, compensated by the memory of her very happy childhood there and she maintained that Brownsea Island was her 'first and last love.'

The School

The 1880 Education Act made attendance at school compulsory for children up to the age of ten. The 1902 Act gave Local Education Authorities the powers to establish secondary and technical schools as well as developing the existing elementary schools. Compulsory education to the age of fourteen years was not introduced until yet another Act in 1918.

Kelly's Directory of 1895 states that there was a National School for 40 children on the island with a Mrs Marsh as the 'Mistress.' The average attendance was given as 36. Six years later, the 1901 census reveals that a Miss Sarah Fooks, age 57, was now the Mistress and that Miss Winfred Foss, her sixteen year old niece, was the Assistant Teacher. Both lived at the School House which, it would appear had originally been a bakery as it had big ovens, although there is no trace of these today.

According to Jack Battrick, in his book *Brownsea Islander,* Miss Fooks 'ruled with a rod of iron' and she left the school in 1904. It would, however, seem that Miss Fooks remained in charge until 1906 as her successor, Miss Henrietta Dunn, was teaching at Arne village school until that year. In the 1923 Kelly's Directory, Miss Dunn was still listed as the Mistress of what was now referred to as Brownsea's Elementary School. At this time in most small schools, there was a Mistress and an Assistant Teacher, the latter often being a bright pupil who had reach school leaving age. This was the case on Brownsea where Louise Campbell (later Mrs Brayley) was Assistant Teacher, according to the records, from 1908-1909 although she maintained that she taught there for six years.

There are only a few surviving school registers but there is evidence that several remained in the school room before Mrs Bonham Christie's death in 1961. The eight registers that do exist are kept at the Dorset County Record Office in Dorchester and they contain the names of 80 different pupils. The Infants' registers show that in December 1911 there were only two pupils. The registers were signed by the Rev. F. S. Algeo in his capacity as 'Manager.' Inevitably, the van Raaltes were influential, with Mrs van Raalte supporting the school financially and involving the children in the island's events such as concerts, plays and pantomimes with her own family and their visitors.

Most of the children at the school were, of course, from the island but some came across each day from the Coastguard Cottages on Sandbanks. These cottages are still there today, in Old Coastguard Road. Other than a few properties 'between the Haven Hotel and the Beehive' (demolished in 2003) Sandbanks consisted, in the early 20th Century, solely of sand dunes so it was easier for the few children living in the area to cross to

School Building

Miss Dunn and the Pupils

Brownsea rather than travel to Poole. They started school at about the age of four although Lily Parker, who lived at the Coastguard Cottages in Sandbanks, was three years and eleven months old in July 1908 and was in the 'Mixed Infants Class.' In April 1908 there were seven children listed in the register but this had risen to fourteen by July. Initially it was an 'all age' school but later some went to secondary school in Poole.

According to Louise Brayley (née Campbell), for six years from about 1909 she took three infants' classes and Miss Dunn took seven classes. The term 'classes' probably means year groups. Mrs Brayley said that there were probably around fifty children in the school at this time. At playtime the children played at the back of the Quay Cottages, but one punishment was to stay in and clean the schoolrooms. Boys left the school at the age of thirteen or fourteen if they were not selected for a Poole Secondary School. Girls left earlier as long as they could read, write and do simple sums!

Alf, Jack And Gwen Toms on the School Steps

The children from Maryland had a mile and a half walk to school and took a packed lunch with them. Often, in the winter, fathers would clear the snow so that the children would have no excuse to stay away from school. On the way home to Maryland they would collect milk in cans from Mrs Pool at the Farm Cottages but this did not stop the children playing hide and seek or in winter, sliding on the ice that covered the East and West Lakes. Mrs Toms blamed the farm workers for the poor quality of the milk but now the truth can be told! Because the children often spilt the milk when they were playing or sliding on the ice, they topped up the cans with water from the lake. They were often hungry after a day at school and would sip the milk from the can before topping it up. They also ate raw turnips from the fields, scraping off most of the dirt and turnip skin on wire fences. They were, apparently, delicious! Other memories of the walk home from school included hearing Miss Margo (as Margherita was known to the islanders) practising her scales in the laundry as they passed by and, when it was, dark being frightened by the calls of the island's deer.

At the beginning of the school day the register was taken, a hymn was sung and there was a Bible reading. Former pupils particularly remembered the school concerts and pantomimes, especially as these involved their parents as well. One year Amy Pool was the pianist, Lily Pond and Lou Campbell took the older parts whilst Vi (Lily Violet) and Daisy Toms were fairies with silvery dresses and crowns, carrying wands covered in tinsel. Daisy sang Buttercups and Daisies as a solo. At the end of the shows, Mrs Pool would give a tea party at her cottage near the farm for all the children who had taken part.

Amy Pool sat for, and won, a scholarship to Poole Technical School. Teaching took place in the reading rooms above the old public library*, but lessons were only held in the mornings. To get to Poole she caught the daily 8 am boat which might be a motor boat with a hood to protect the passengers in rough weather, a sailing boat or often the steam launch *Blunderbuss* skippered by Tom Dean. As someone who could both row and sail, Amy preferred the sailing boat, and she was allowed to steer through Half Diver and the channels. The return trip to Brownsea was more chancy. Sometimes she travelled with the Water Postman, a Mr Blundell, who used a duck-punt when the weather was calm. If Amy knew there was a boat coming across in the afternoon she would wait for it in the reading room of the Mission for Seamen on Poole Quay which was run, she remembered, by a Mr Joseph Andrews. Frequently no boat was available so she would walk to Sandbanks and catch the coastguard boat which went across to collect the coastguards'

* *Poole Technical and Commercial School was at Mount Street, now at the end of Lagland Street.*

children attending the Brownsea School. Amy's mother, Mrs Pool, was not happy living on Brownsea for the tide was very strong, even on a calm day, and sometimes it was dark when the children were coming home across the water. She would always pray for their safe return.

Once a week, Amy had piano lessons in Bournemouth On that day, after leaving school at noon, she would catch the tram to County Gates, and then walk to the Music Master's house. After the lesson she would walk back to County Gates and then through Branksome Woods to Sandbanks. There was no main road, except through Martello Road, and her route was through paths covered with pine needles and then over the rough hills to Sandbanks Road. One day, when Amy realised that the weather was too rough for her father to come and fetch her, she spent the night in a coastguard house and, next morning, walked back to her school in Poole. After a year or two, the Technical School was discontinued so she attended the Secondary School near Park Gates. This was an all-day school and later became the co-educational Parkstone Grammar School. As a result of her daily appearances on Poole Quay Amy was known to the fishermen and workers on the quay as 'Grace Darling', after the lifeboat heroine of 1838. Later she became a pupil-teacher at a school in Oakdale and by this time, her brother Leonard was also attending a Secondary School.

Education was obviously rather different for the van Raalte children. Noel was sent to Eton, and Margherita, at fifteen, was also sent away to a private boarding school, St James, in London. It was housed in a large Italian style villa with cloisters. She had by now overcome her shyness and on her first day at the school she dropped a bully over the balustrade into the rose bushes. The girls at the school were up to all kinds of escapades

School Concert

and were severely admonished if they were caught 'out of bounds.' Margherita managed never to get caught but here escapades included sleeping on the flat roof and swimming in the fish ponds. She even bribed a gardener so that she could go rabbit shooting in the evenings, but had to climb a drainpipe to get back into the dormitory.

At the end of her first term at the school Margherita was chosen for the star part of 'Princess Zara' in a musical. Many girls who had already spent four terms at the school were jealous of her success in winning the part. When the Infanta Eulalie of Spain wrote to Margherita to tell her that a member of the royal family would be visiting her at the school, she had to teach four of the teachers how to curtsy. They were all tall women, ranging in height from six feet two inches to six feet four inches, but they managed a passable curtsy when the royal visitor (who was 'covered in bracelets') arrived.

On leaving St James', Margherita studied at the Royal College of Music, but was there for only one year. She wanted to transfer to the Slade School of Painting but received 'an adamant refusal' from her mother.

According to Margherita, 'Poots (Gwen) went to Heathfield School for a few terms but they did not appreciate her there!' Apparently her main offence was writing fan-mail letters to well known actors such as Gerald du Maurier. She was then sent to Margherita's old boarding school, St James, where, because she was very small and a fast runner, was immediately put into the hockey First Eleven.

Mrs van Raalte with Gwen, left, and Margherita

56

The Church and Christmas Activities

An important feature of life on Brownsea was its church, St Mary's*, which was built during Colonel Waugh's ownership of Brownsea and consecrated in 1854. George Cavendish Bentinck, Brownsea's owner from 1873 until 1890, added several valuable 16th to 18th century artefacts including a pair of brass hanging candelabra, altar candlesticks from a Benedictine Monastery near Padua and two marble statues of angels from Venice. From 1895 it was the responsibility of the Rev. Frederick Swift Algeo (nicknamed 'Holy Joe' by the islanders) and he conducted the services on Sunday afternoons. He was Vicar of Studland and he would walk along the beach from his vicarage, a distance of more than two miles, to the point where he would be picked up by the island launch. From 1901, after the service, he would 'take afternoon tea' with Mr and Mrs van Raalte before being taken back to the mainland. If the weather was too rough for him to cross to the island, the head gardener, Mr Fred Pool and later, Mr Alfred Campbell the estate carpenter and bandmaster, would take the service.

As in all villages throughout England it was the custom for all the islanders to attend the Sunday service, although it was noted in one report that one family 'never went to church.' St Mary's could accommodate 70 or 80 people and Mr and Mrs van Raalte and any guests who were there that weekend would come to the service. The guests would sit with the islanders whilst Mr and Mrs van Raalte would sit in the family pews at the rear, west end of the church, thus avoiding a parade down the aisle to the front in the manner of so many estate owners. On cold days the back of the church was heated by an open fire which can still be seen. This area was furnished with carpets, lounge chairs and small desks to hold hymn and service books. It was very dark as there was wooden panelling on both sides. Later, after Charles van Raalte's death, a chapel was built with a window on the south side. On dark days, the lit candles in the candelabra (still in position today) would have given some light.

Naturally, the church had a belfry. There were four bells and the belfry had a fire for the ringers, directly above the one in the church. The ubiquitous Fred Pool was a bell ringer, choirmaster and organist, as well as being leader of the temperance organisation, the Band of Hope. Alfred Campbell was another choirmaster and organist, and was, at times, a bell ringer. Other organists were Louise Campbell and Gwen Toms. Fred Toms was churchwarden and he was also the sexton. When Mr and Mrs van Raalte and their guests arrived at the church, a cord was pulled which rang a small bell in the bell tower.

* Much of the information about the church was provided by Dot Orchard, and it was collated by her daughter, Janet Mellors

This was a signal for the ringers to stop and to take their place in the main body of the church. Often, one of them would double as organist. The bells were re-cast in 1988 and four more were installed, making eight in total.

Living on an island meant that there were difficulties in performing a number of routine tasks, such a registering a birth or a death. For Brownsea the Registrar's Office was in Swanage which meant that the informant had to cross by boat to Studland and then walk all along the beach to that seaside town. Occasionally the Registrar would come to Studland, but such arrangements had to be agreed by post before this would happen.

From time to time children were confirmed at the church. In November 1906, Vincent R. Ryan, the Bishop of Salisbury, came to St Mary's to confirm Noel van Raalte, Harry Dean, William Dean, Emily Dean, Emily Bradley, Esther Jane (Jinny) Biggs and five others. The Rector of St James, Poole, the Rev R Fawkes and the Rev FS Algeo were also there, probably because of the Bishop's presence. Weddings, funerals and burials in the churchyard were also held at the church and full lists of those involved are available on the island (in the Visitor Centre). Infant mortality was high and island families were not immune to some of the virulent diseases of the mainland.

Christmas celebrations on Brownsea involved the church, school and castle. Gwen Toms remembered school concerts and the pupils' mothers making the dresses, especially the Japanese ones that they wore when she was eight years old. In 1904, when Daisy Toms was about eleven, several visitors joined the islanders in their pantomime. After each rehearsal the islanders were invited to tea at the castle in the servants' dining room. At the end of the show a flashlight photograph was taken and presented to all the performers

The Church before 1908

58

The Pantomime
1. *Daisy Toms, 2. Jinny Biggs, 3. Nellie Hyde, 4. Noel van Raalte,*
5. Lord Elliot, 6. Sir Henry Colville, 7. Marguerite van Raalte,
8. Gwendoline van Raalte, 9. Lily Pool, 10. Ronald Cobb,
11. Make-Up Lady (Unknown), 12. Mr. Cobb, 13. Louise Campbell, 14. Mr. Campbell.

and behind-the-scenes staff. Mr Cobb was the electrician and Mr Campbell made and fixed the scenery. In the castle, the children were amazed at large and beautiful rooms, the 'wonderful' hanging tapestries, the wide, carpeted staircases and all the musical instruments on display.

Each Christmas the Toms children received an apple, an orange, nuts and sweets in a stocking but other presents were limited, particularly when compared with those received by children today! On one occasion Daisy had a doll and she showed it to her younger brother Jack. He accidentally dropped it and the head was broken. However, 'Father Christmas' brought her a new one a few days later. Daisy and Vi were always making new clothes for their dolls and in later life became dressmakers and tailors on the mainland.

Each year Mr and Mrs van Raalte held a Christmas party for the islanders at the castle where gifts were taken from the Christmas tree and handed out. Daisy Toms remembered a year when Guglielmo Marconi and Miss Beatrice O'Brien, before they were married, handed out the presents. She had to shake Mr Marconi's hand and curtsy to Miss O'Brien. All the islanders ate in the castle's dining room, and the meal was followed by a dance and singsong. One Christmas Daisy sang *Meet me Tonight in Dreamland* accompanied at the piano by Nellie Hyde. Every family received a brace of pheasants, a rabbit and a Christmas pudding from Mr and Mrs van Raalte.

The Death of Charles van Raalte

Charles van Raalte was obviously a very disappointed man in the months following his failure to win a seat in Parliament in the general election of 1906. In order to refresh his spirits, he and Mrs van Raalte planned a six month cruise to the East beginning in1907 and returning home in 1908 in time for Margherita's coming-out season. Their itinerary included Egypt, Ceylon and Burma, returning home via India. They sailed on a P & O ship but Margherita, who appears to have been the only one of the three van Raalte

Mr van Raalte's tomb
Likeness to Mr van Raalte

children to make the trip, described the conditions on board as 'filthy' and said 'bad water' was used for cooking. She also said that sixteen 'natives' died during the voyage and their bodies thrown overboard.

The weather became so hot during the voyage that Charles van Raalte slept on deck but in the evening there were heavy mists and his clothes became damp. By the time they reached India he was seriously ill. He was taken to hospital in Calcutta and died there three days later with a chill on his kidneys and pneumonia on 31 December 1907. He was 50 years old. Florence and Margherita returned home grief stricken and in deep mourning. The hotel manager in Calcutta where the ladies were staying was, like Charles van Raalte, a Freemason and he arranged for the body to be embalmed and returned to Brownsea Island in February 1908. There the grief stricken islanders awaited the return of their popular 'Squire.'

A path was made across Home Field, then just a hay field, for the bier, made by Alfred Campbell the estate carpenter, to carry the coffin from the castle to St Mary's Church. On 11 February 1908 a quiet family funeral was conducted by the Rev. Frederick Algeo. Florence van Raalte wanted Charles to be buried inside the church but this was not allowed, so he was buried just outside the church, on the south side adjacent to the wall of the family pew. Soon afterwards, a 'faculty' or authorisation was obtained for a memorial chapel or mausoleum to be built. The south side of the family pew was opened up and the chapel built. Florence van Raalte commissioned an effigy of Charles to be made in marble and this took up most of the chapel. No expense was spared and the commission was given to Alfred Drury (1857-1944) who was one of the most eminent and fashionable sculptors of the time. Those who knew Charles van Raalte commented that the effigy was a marvellous likeness.

The Latin inscription on the tomb is

IN

BONAM MEMORIAM

CAROLI VAN RAALTE

DE INSULA BROWNSEA QVI NATVS

AD MDCCCLVII OBIIT AD MCMVII

HOC MONVMENTVM POSVIT CONJVX

EJVX DEVOTISSIMA FLORENTIA

translated as

To the worthy memory of Charles van Raalte of Brownsea Island who was born AD1857 and died AD1907. His most devoted wife Florence set up this monument.

On the inscription BONAM translated literally is good. Cicero, in his writing, uses boni to refer to honest, honourable men. The carving has one error – EJUX should read EJUS – but this may be acceptable for an engraving.

The mausoleum had a screen, carved by Alfred Campbell, which had been copied from the one in the family pew and was much admired by Mrs van Raalte. The family

The Church after 1908 (taken 2004) with the extension for Mr van Raalte's Tomb

pew now had a window on the south side and this made it appreciably lighter. Another memorial was produced by Carter Tiles of Poole in 1907 with their turquoise blue tile featuring a shadowy portrait of Charles van Raalte. This was sold in aid of the League of Help which organised assistance for the unemployed and destitute of Poole.

One piece of good news that delighted the islanders was that Florence van Raalte was not going to leave or sell Brownsea but would continue to entertain her guests there. Her son, Noel, was approaching twenty years of age, and had assumed that he would take over many of his father's responsibilities. It was reported that Noel was left a 'vast' fortune by his father, and was later left £1,000,000 by his Dutch grandfather. Florence encouraged him in his new role as head of the family and agreed that he should partly manage the estate and arrange special shooting parties. However, she often countermanded his orders and arrangements which made Noel very angry, and he would retreat into his workshop. Because of her father's death, Margherita's coming out was postponed until 1909, when she was nineteen.

In the Spring of 1908 Florence went on a painting holiday to the Isles of Scilly and it was there that she saw the fields of daffodils which were an important part of the local economy. She decided to introduce daffodil growing to Brownsea Island, a decision that would give more work over a longer period of the year for the islanders and thus maintain the strength of the island band! She managed to persuade the son of the daffodil growing manager on the Scilly Island of Tresco to come to Brownsea as Steward. As his name was William Brown, he was known on Brownsea as 'Tresco' Brown to avoid confusion with George Brown the Head Gardener at that time.

After a few years, fourteen acres of the island were under daffodil and narcissi cultivation. Louise Campbell (later Brayley) was not allowed to help with the flowers as her father said that it was 'too tiring' but this was probably an excuse to prevent her doing work that was considered too menial for the daughter of the Head Estate Carpenter. However, she later described the procedures used in the island's new 'industry.' Her father made divisions which fitted into a cart so that the daffodils could be carried upright for delivery each day to various homes where they would be tied into bunches of twelve. Jack Battrick said that an average 750 bunches were tied each night. All the families on the island were involved and received tenpence (or about 4p in today's money) for each hundred tied bundles. Lou Campbell added that the daffodils were taken to what is now the Visitors' Centre and plunged into buckets of water. The blooms were then packed into boxes and sent, six days a week, to London's Covent Garden.

Getting the blooms to London started with the crossing by launch to Sandbanks where they were collected by John Hayes who lived in the house adjoining the stables on the mainland. 'Johnny', as he was known, had come with the van Raaltes from London when they bought Brownsea. From Sandbanks the daffodils went to Bournemouth Railway Station and by train to London. Some, later, reports have them being put on the train at Poole. Because of the mild climate in the interior of the island, it was found that the Brownsea daffodils were second only to those of the Scilly Isles in being ready for the market and ahead of the blooms from Cambridgeshire and Lincolnshire.

Not all the daffodils were sent to London. Many were used for decorating the castle

Daffodil Industry

rooms, including those used by guests. In the autumn, some of the bulbs were harvested and sold with the better bulbs fetching, according to Jack Battrick, up to £90 a ton. During the winter, boxes were made, ready for the next season. Among the varieties of daffodils grown on Brownsea, and remembered by Jack Battrick, were Grand Monarch, Scilling Whites, Sir Watkin and Glory of Seyden. Chappie Chapman added that there was also 'White Pheasant-eye.' Apparently there are 26,000 recorded varieties of daffodil and narcissi!

The daffodils were not Mrs van Raalte's only horticultural innovation in the years after her husband's death. She sent the Head Gardener, George Brown, to Kew Gardens to get ideas for establishing a sunken garden on Brownsea. Lou Campbell described the end result as a beautiful sunken garden with a raised wall, shrubs and eucalyptus trees in front of the castle. She also remembered that there were raised tennis courts, and hydrangea and lavender walks. Although Charles' death was a tragedy, his widow was clearly determine to continue his work in making Brownsea a family retreat and a place 'in the country' to entertain her High Society guests.

Florence van Raalte Alone

Royalty continued to be entertained at the castle after Charles van Raalte's death. If it was known that a group of visitors would be walking through the farm, special attention was paid to cleanliness in the cowshed so that the long dresses worn by the ladies were not dirtied. On one occasion Prince Alfonso of Spain, with his three sons, the Queen of Romania and her two sons and her daughter Princess Elina, and Prince Paul of Bulgaria were all in the cowshed watching Princess Alphonso and Lady Howard de Walden being taught to milk a cow. The two ladies quickly learnt the art!

In 1909, whilst on holiday in Spain with her mother, Margherita was taken ill. She was left with a only a maid to look after her while the others in the party continued their sightseeing further afield. Margherita recovered and was accompanied by Luis, the Infante of Orleans Bourbon, to night clubs and on sightseeing trips. In a cathedral she was thrilled by the brilliance of the organ playing. However, the holiday was brought to an abrupt end when Mrs van Raalte received a telegram telling her that 59 year old John Hayes had died of influenza. This was the man who oversaw the sending of the daffodils to London and had been employed by the van Raaltes for over thirty years. 'Johnny' had been head coachman when they had lived in Grosvenor Square.

Mrs van Raalte and Margherita returned for his funeral which was held in St Mary's Church in April 1909. His obituary was published in the Poole Herald of 8 April 1909 under the heading 'Death of the Steward' and it referred to the many works of improvement that had been carried out on Brownsea Island under his supervision and that he was known in Poole, particularly as a result of his efforts on behalf of Charles van Raalte during his election campaigns. It says much for the good relationship that existed between the upper class van Raaltes and their staff that Florence and Margherita should travel across Europe to attend the funeral of their former steward.

Life changed for Margherita in 1912 when she married Tommy Ellis, 8th Lord Howard de Walden and 4th Lord Seaford. He was about ten years her senior and owned vast properties in London, properties that he had inherited from his grandmother, a Cavendish Bentinck. These totalled 100 acres and were mainly in central London and included Harley Street and Wimpole Street which were 'conservatively valued at £250 million.' His parents had been friends of the van Raaltes for many years and were regular visitors to Brownsea, occasionally renting Furzey Island. Tommy and Margherita did not want any fuss and their London wedding was held two days earlier than had originally been planned. Because of this change only 30 guests were present rather than the 500 who had hoped or expected to be there!

Mrs van Raalte at Margherita's Wedding

The wedding present from the van Raaltes' tenants on Brownsea Island was a silver inkstand and it was displayed in the window of Hansford's, a jewellers' shop in Poole High Street. It was inscribed with the date of the wedding, 20 January 1912, but this was, thanks to the change in plans by the young couple, wrong by two days. Lord de Walden's present to his bride was a diamond necklace, and to each of the ladies who had attended the select ceremony he gave a diamond brooch, and to each man, a diamond tie clip. Even with his wealth, it would have been very costly for him to provide such gifts to 500 guests! A newspaper report states that Mrs van Raalte gave a reception 'on the afternoon of the wedding' but adds, surprisingly, that the guests had no idea that the marriage service had already taken place.

For the children of Brownsea the wedding was doubly exciting for it gave them a day off school and a special celebration tea. More than 100 youngsters were each given a mug with pictures of the de Waldens painted on them. It is not known whether any of these mugs survive.

Two years later Britain was at war and the Great War brought much sadness to Brownsea Island. One report states that at the outbreak of war on 4 August 1914 Noel van Raalte and four of the island's men volunteered. Certainly a large number of men from Brownsea enlisted with Noel being put on coastal patrol duties. He survived the

Islanders off to War (Coal Boat in the background)

war. Some men were sent directly to the front line and, according to Jack Battrick, nearly thirty men volunteered or were called when conscription was introduced in 1916. Of these, only six returned to Brownsea but in a number of cases this was because they chose to live and work elsewhere.

A memorial plaque to those who lost their lives was put up, apparently, on the wall near the quay, adjacent to the double gates.* It was thought to be of wooden construction but no trace of it can now be found. Jack Battrick said that among the names were:

Robert (Bob) Martin Biggs – torpedoed in the Atlantic, rescued, but then died

(Alfred James) Christian Biggs – died in France, March 1918

Joseph Thomas Dean – died in France March 1918

Fred Dean – died at the Battle of the Somme, July 1916

Herbert John Sticklin – died at Gallipoli, August 1915

John Tizzard – died in India September 1919, probably from Malaria

* *Letter to Mrs Dot Orchard, February 1996, from the Ordnance Survey*

George and Charles Toms, Mr Northover in Army uniform, at the Daffodil Fields

Mrs van Raalte went to great lengths to assist the wounded or to offer her condolences to the families of those who died. 'Tiny' Goddard, who had been injured at Gallipoli, was eventually brought home to Brownsea but he had shrapnel embedded in his feet and could only work with difficulty. Mrs van Raalte helped to nurse him back to health and then was able to offer him his old job. Arthur Northover survived, having been awarded the Croix de Guerre for bringing a wounded French officer back from no-mans-land.

The island itself was affected by the war for vast areas of trees were cut down to provide pit props for the trenches in France. Two huts were built east of Maryland village for the workmen and their horses and, when the war was over, these were used for dances and for daffodil storage and sorting. On one occasion, twenty minesweepers left the harbour under full steam and their wash caused considerable flooding around the quay. C.J. Biggs also mentioned this incident but in his version there was a flotilla of thirteen destroyers leaving in line astern on a very high spring tide, forcing water into the front and out of the back of the Quay Cottages.

Whilst working in Portsmouth, Daisy Toms met Arthur Chapman, a sailor based in Portsmouth, and in 1913 they were engaged to be married. One weekend Daisy and Arthur were sitting on Pottery Pier when Alf Toms brought across a telegram instructing Arthur to report to HMS Fearless at Portsmouth. The tide was out and soon the rowing boat carrying Arthur, Daisy and Alf was stuck in the mud. The two men removed their shoes, rolled up their trousers and jumped into the water and, with Daisy using an oar and Arthur and Alf pushing, managed to reach deeper water. Both men were covered in slime and although Arthur reached the railway station just in time, he was unable to clean himself up before departing.

The Gardens
Brownsea Island
Poole. Dorset:
1st Jan. 1924

This is to certify that
Olive Bromfield has
been employed under
me in these gardens,
first in the Kitchen gdn.
from Jan. 1916 to Jan.
1917 - and after serving
2 years in H. M. Forces,
he returned in Jan. 1919
and during the 5 years
to present date, has
assisted a man with
the glass.
I have always found

him very attentive to
his duties, and interested
in his work, very civil
and obliging.
He leaves here to gain
further knowledge, and
I can recommend him
to any one requiring a
steady, sober and
reliable young man.
I shall be pleased
at any time to answer
any enquiries concerning
him.

Signed.
George Brown,
Hd. Gardener to
Mr C. Van Raalte
Brownsea Castle
Poole

Reference for Oliver Broomfield who returned after the war.

Arthur Chapman was wounded in the naval battles at Heligoland and whilst he was convalescing at Chatham, he and Daisy were married there. When Daisy became pregnant she returned to Brownsea. Mrs Toms had assisted at several births on the island, many of them when the doctor, having to come from Poole, did not arrive in time. Daisy was fortunate in that the doctor, who was visiting a patient in Maryland, came to see her because she had tripped and sprained her ankle. The baby was not due for a fortnight and the doctor said he would return to Poole as there was no urgency. Mrs Toms disagreed and persuaded the doctor to sleep on the sofa and at midnight a boy, Melvin but always known as Chappie or Chap, was born. It was lucky that the doctor was present as Daisy had violent pains in her legs and he said that in order to avoid permanent injury she should immediately start walking around the house.

After the war, Daisy, Arthur and Chappie moved away from the island. As he grew up Chappie spent many holidays at his grandparents' home on Brownsea Island, accompanied by his friend Lew. Many of their activities would be frowned upon today, if not banned because of safety considerations. Chappie remembered riding perched on the side of a cart pulled by a horse with Grandfather Toms. He and Lew climbed and slid on the cliffs, dug holes to hide in, and used clay to make dens. The areas around the brick shaft below Seymour's Cottage, used in the 19th Century to extract clay, were-out-of bounds but the children did not think that they were dangerous. How wrong they were, for some of the shafts are over 60 feet deep! In 1963, when Chappie joined the group of volunteers to protect the island after Mrs Bonham Christie's death, some of his clay 'building and tunnelling operations of the 1920s' were still to be seen.

When the war was over George Toms became Head Gardener, and he left the Bothy when he married and went to live at Seymours. The Toms family were normally very house-proud but this was not the case with George and his wife Gert. Their garden was over-run with chickens and 'they even went into the house.' They had a brick built shed with a boiler for boiling the chicken feed. Nearby there was a brick built toilet, shaped like a circular pillar box which had been built in this form to accommodate the ladies and their hooped skirts. It was often used by the ladies from the castle when they were riding round the island in a pony and trap.

Top: Seymours Cottage

Remains of Seymours Cottage (1975)

Remains of the Circular Toilet

Chappie and Lew at Play

There was a great deal of support within the family to bring up the large number of children and, if someone was ill, other islanders would 'rally round' and help. Even May Brown, the wife of 'Tresco' the Island Steward, who was considered to be rather aloof, helped at times. During the war Mrs Toms had been ill with a 'floating tumour' in her stomach and, after some treatment, the doctor said it was serious and gave her only six months to live. When Mrs van Raalte heard of this she said, 'Nonsense, we must not let her die.' She knew the President of St Mary's Hospital in London and arranged for Alice Toms to be admitted to the hospital in August 1916. The Sister in charge of the ward had been instructed to treat her as 'a special case and not let her die.' She was operated on and lived for another nineteen years and frequently went swimming off Maryland during the majority of those years. The hospital costs were completely covered by Mrs van Raalte, who often drove her pony and trap to see her at Maryland. Later, when Mrs van Raalte heard that Mr Toms, then living in Parkstone, was ill, she sent him a cheque and instructed the island doctor to get him fit again.

Highlights of life in Maryland at this time were the free dancing lessons given by Fred and Alice Toms who had been keen on dancing in their younger days. The largest room , the one which contained the built-in copper for boiling clothes and Christmas puddings and which was now mainly used as a storeroom, was cleared and Mr Toms and Mr Mackrell played violins, whilst another man played a concertina. In the intervals they all sang amusing songs. The children, who had dancing classes on a different night, were allowed to sit and watch. After the war, one of the huts built by the forestry workers during the war was used for dancing. The Toms family were good musicians, and could play several instruments. Mr Toms and four of his sons were in the Island Band. During the Great War Charles Toms conducted a regimental band and did all the arranging and,

Mrs van Raalte's Trap (photo taken 1962)

after the war, he had his own orchestra and held dancing classes.

One of the most important links with mainland was the postman. He maintained a vital service, delivering letters and parcels, and emptied the island's pillar box on the Quay, the same one that is used today. He would take children to and from school if they missed the island launch, or there was not one due. He would also collect groceries or other goods by arrangement from Newman's Boat Yard, to take to the island. Even in very rough weather, he seldom missed a delivery.

One of these 'water postmen' was Billy Blundell who would row or sail across, using a duck punt in calm weather. Fred Pool mentioned that as the children were proficient sailors, Billy would sometimes let the youngsters sail his boat and he would settle himself down and read a novel. On one occasion, when the boat went aground, they were stranded for two hours and, as the water was so low, they climbed out of the boat and played a game of cricket on the sand bank!

Another 'water postman' was George Blackmore and he had this role from 1919 until 1924. He was interviewed in 1979, when he was about 80 years old, and told how he used his own boat, a 12 feet lugsail broad beam, which he sailed or rowed from Poole Quay. He was paid ten shillings a week extra for using his own boat. He would leave his Poole canoe, which he sometimes used to go to the other islands, anchored off Maryland with the oars and the rowlocks hidden in a hedge. As he said, when pointing out that they had never been stolen – 'You could not do that today!'

George Blackmore would deliver mail to all houses on the island although the majority of it was for the castle. One day he pulled up to Brownsea Quay with a large number of sacks containing both parcels and letters. A man who was fishing from the quay put down his rod and in broken English said, 'You are laden this morning, I will help.' He assisted in the loading of the truck which was left on the quay for deliveries to the castle and helped push it to the castle. After unloading the truck the footman called the postman aside and said to him, 'Do you know that your helper was Prince Olaf of Norway?' He later became King Olaf of Norway.

Mr Blackmore also remembered 'dare-devil' Noel van Raalte driving his car fast on the island's gravel or pine covered tracks. Older people would say to the postman, 'He's going straight into one of those trees one of these nights.' Noel was also remembered as a driver of fast motor boats, particularly as most of the boats in the harbour still had sails or oars. One day Noel van Raalte offered to tow the postman's boat back to Poole. George Blackmore was reluctant to pass the rope to him but Noel, with a smile, said, 'I'll not go fast – just crawling up the harbour' and he was passed the rope. By the time they reached Half Diver buoy the rope had to be slackened to stop the stern of the postman's boat from going under.

End of an Era

Noel van Raalte was to marry three times, and first marriage was to a niece of the Duke of Montrose, Iris Graham. To start with they lived on Brownsea, at the Villa which had been extended. To look after them they employed Jinny and May Biggs, who clearly spread the word around that Noel and his young wife bathed together. Apparently they made a lot of noise and there was a lot of water for the servants to clear up. Their first child, a daughter named Gonda was christened in St Mary's church in March 1914. In the register Noel is recorded as a 'Gentleman.' An explanation of the little girl's unusual Christian name is that Noel owned a Lagonda car at the time! Later Noel and Iris left Brownsea and moved to Bursledon, in Hampshire, where he built boats. They had a second daughter, Charmain but the marriage ended in divorce. His second marriage was to a lady named Beryl Gibbons and they had a son, Harry. He married for the third time and died at the age of 49 from duodenal ulcers.

Life on Brownsea was never insular, for there were always changes bought about by necessity or curiosity. Many of the island children, on leaving school, found work on the island but some went to the mainland instead. On occasions, some left to become servants to people who had been guests on the island. In 1919 or 1920 Gwen Toms and Mr Fisher, the butler, went to work in London, at Mrs van Raalte's Park Lane flat. Some were able to follow up the interests they had developed on the island. Jack and Alf Toms, for instance, joined the Marine School of Music whilst Charles Toms, who had been apprenticed as a carpenter with Mr Campbell, went to Canada in 1913. He joined the Canadian Army when war broke out a year later. He came back to Poole after the war, working at the Poole Gas Works, and married the islander May Biggs in December 1920. His interest in music was life-long and when he died in 1950 he asked to be buried with his silver cornet. Daisy and Vi Toms, who in their younger days were always making clothes for their dolls, became dressmakers and tailors in Portsmouth, where Daisy met her future husband. As apprentices their pay was a shilling a week in the first year, doubling in the second. Later they lived with their sister Mabel in Poole and travelled daily to work as dressmakers and tailors at Vaneks in Bournemouth. Each weekend was spent at home, on Brownsea Island!

Mrs van Raalte continued to hold parties and shooting weekends but they became fewer and fewer. Margherita and her husband assisted in the running of the island and often leased Furzey Island, as their main home was Chirk Castle in North Wales. Lord Howard de Walden bought some Eland deer from Africa for the Chirk Castle estate and had them quarantined on Brownsea. New fences were erected especially for them. The

Lady Margherita Howard de Walden and her six Children

'water postman' George Blackmore said that on the day after their arrival all the fences had gone, along with the wire and the deer themselves! Their long, straight horns had lifted all the fencing out of the grounds and the deer were found on Furzey Island.

Margherita remembered the time when she had six children and they leased Furzey Island. It was quite barren, with bracken, heather and a few stunted trees and had a bungalow for the living accommodation. The landing stage was long and double planked over the mud flats. Harry Dean, son of the 'old' boatman, 'looked after' the family when they were on Furzey. The de Walden children had great fun during their times on Furzey Island and it took an hour to clean them up before visiting their grandmother on Brownsea Island. Florence van Raalte usually had a house full, with many of her guests being rather important people. So that the daughters knew when to curtsy to foreign royalty, Margherita, like her mother when she was a child, would signal by pretending to brush a wasp from her face.

Margherita's six children were five girls and one boy, John, born in November 1912, who later became the 9th Baron de Walden. It is interesting to note that John could, in theory, have prevented the Second World War from happening for, when he was in Munich as a language student in 1931, he hit a pedestrian whilst driving his car. That pedestrian was Aldolf Hitler. However, he survived the accident as he was only slightly hurt! Some years later, when John was at the opera in Munich, he was seated in a box next to the Fuehrer. He leaned across and asked Hitler if he remembered the incident. 'He did remember the incident and we had a charming conversation for a few moments, never to meet again.'

Margherita had an interesting and eventful life. She supported theatrical and musical productions and even instigated the annual Queen Charlotte Ball. During the First World

Daffodils still blooming (photo 2003)

Restored farm carts and machinery (photo 2005)

Newspaper Cutting of the 1927 Sale

Among the thousands of lots to go under the hammer were many musical instruments which went at very low prices.

A French musette of 1700 in a leather bag covered with green velvet and old silver lace, with ivory chanter and side drone, each with six silver keys, fetched £8.

A triple flagelot, by Bainbridge of London, probably made in 1820, went for £7 15s. An early 19th century tabor pipe sold for £6 15s.

The pipe belonged to Thomas Humphries, of Oxfordshire, and was played by him at most of the Morris dances in the villages and towns of this county for nearly 40 years.

Seventeenth century lutes were sold for £5 and an Italian mandolin of 1777 for five guineas.

The Corridor after the 1927 Sale

78

War she set up a hospital in Egypt for casualties from Gallipoli. This was because the war was not going well in that part of the world and she had to use her influence to hold the injured soldiers until they were fit enough to return to the front line. She had a particular interest in this aspect of the fighting for her husband was second-in-command of the Westminster Dragoons and they had been sent to Egypt early in the war. Lord Howard de Walden saw action in Gallipoli with a Welsh regiment and also served in France. Margherita set up the Howard de Walden Maternity Home for the wives of officers in London and on the birth of her fifth child, received a silver clock from '336 grateful mothers.' In 1920 she was awarded the CBE.

Eventually, in 1925, Florence van Raalte decided to sell Brownsea Island and Sir Arthur Wheeler, who owned the Haven Hotel, bought it for £62,000. Mrs van Raalte left most of the contents of the castle and farm, and these were included in the sale. One mystery from this sale was the fate of Charles van Raalte's fabulous collection of musical instruments, with many believing that they were taken to Lord and Lady de Walden's home at Chirk Castle and then to Dean Castle in Ayrshire which the family had inherited in the first years of the twentieth century. In 1975 Dean castle was gifted 'to the Burgh of Kilmarnock by John, 9th Lord Howard de Walden, along with the 8th Lord Howard's collection of arms and armour, and the van Raalte collection of musical instruments.'

However, when Sir Arthur Wheeler failed to get permission to develop Brownsea

The Church and Church Field 2004

Island, he decided to sell it. Fox and Sons were the auctioneers for the sale (which lasted nine days) of 2,715 items from the castle. From the sales catalogue and the auctioneers' papers it seems that over 200 musical instruments were included in the sale and some were sold for less than the price of kitchen utensils.* The 91 musical instruments at Dean Castle† are thought to have been taken from Brownsea by Margherita when Mrs van Raalte decided to sell the island in 1925.

The quarter century that Brownsea was owned by the van Raaltes can clearly be regarded as the island's 'golden age.' It was possibly one or the most unusual estates in southern England but the family ran it in the grand manner befitting the Edwardian upper classes. They were benevolent employers and extremely generous hosts to their many, many visitors. It is always tempting to view the past through rose coloured glasses but it does seem that everyone living on Brownsea during the van Raalte years led a happier and healthier life than many of their contemporaries on the mainland. All this was to change when, following Sir Arthur Wheeler's short ownership, Brownsea was sold in 1927 to Mrs Bonham Christie for £125,000, approximately double the price he had paid. The details of her long ownership are recounted in the book *For Nature Not Humans* by the author of this work, and they tell a completely different story!

* See Appendices A
† See website www.futuremuseum.co.uk

Good - Bye !

Three things I ask of you before we part,
  One little corner for me in your heart?
One thought of me in every passing day
One tiny prayer for me. when 'er you pray.

And so - Good bye -
Yet. friendship's. Chain
Will hold us fast until we meet again
For over all the leagues of land and sea
My thoughts will pass to you.
  And yours to me.

A. E. Campbell.
Bryher Island
April 23rd
1928

*Goodbye entry from Alfred Campbell in May Brown's Autograph
Book when she and Tresco were leaving the Island*

Appendix A

The 1927 Auction and Sale

The contents of the Castle were sold in 2715 Lots on Brownsea Island over nine days by the auctioneers Fox & Sons on the instructions of Sir Arthur Wheeler, owner of the Island from 1925 to 1927. Some of the items in the sale had been brought to Brownsea by previous owners but the vast majority by Charles and Florence van Raalte.

In The National Trust's Brownsea Archive are the sale prices of Lots 1 to 832 and 1721 to 2715, with the names of the purchasers. This Appendix shows a typical double page from the Auctioneer's notes and a few more descriptions with purchasers' names and the prices paid.

Copies of more pages from the auctioneer's notes including Lots 1721 to 1927, the musical instruments, are not included in this book, but can be seen at The National Trust Visitor Centre, Brownsea Island, or at the Poole Local History Centre at Poole Museum in the High Street during normal opening times.

The Auctioneer's two notebooks, the third being missing, containing details of Lots 1 to 832 and 1721 to 2715 can be viewed by prior appointment with The National Trust, Brownsea Island, usually from April to October. A fee may be payable.

651   A 4ft. 6in white enamelled Adam style bedstead with head and foot panels in silk tapestry, the canopy over with two pairs of lines silk tapestry curtains with valence *Cargill £5.0.0*

652   A 6ft hair stuffed box spring mattress with wooden wedge, on deal frame and supports *do., £1.16.0*

653   A 6ft excellent hair mattress *do., £3.5.0*

654   Small leather bolster, two down pillows, Marcella counterpane and dimity valance *Lenaine £2.8.0*

655   A large good quality blanket and two single bed ditto *Lenaine £2.4.0*

656   An eiderdown in pink silk case *Brown £2.6.0*

657   A 7ft carved white enamelled right-arm couch with scroll foot, spring and hair stiffed, and covered in silk damask and loose cretonne cover *Taylor £2.10.0*

658   Wicker easy arm chair, spring stuffed and upholstered in tapestry *George £1.8.0*

659   An 18in well-made mahogany 3-division music Canterbury, fitted drawer *Fredericks £2.6.0*

660   A 20in mahogany circular table with undertier on tapered supports *Greenmond £1.1.0*

661   A 27in Sheridan mahogany and inlaid Corner Washstand, with undertier and fitted drawer *Jenkins £5.0.0*

662   A 23in ditto *George £5.10.0*

663   An antique mahogany and inlaid ebony Cheval Glass, plate 20in by 38in *Fredericks £12.10.0*

664   A 2ft 9in ANTIQUE MAHOGANY INLAID SOFA TABLE fitted two drawers, on four shaped legs and brass claw feet *Ford & Co £17.0.0*

665   An attractive mahogany and inlaid swing toilet mirror, oval plate, 19in by 14in *Greenmond £2.4.0*

666   A 6ft four-fold draught screen with panels in tapestry *West Mr £1.6.0*

667   THE ELEGANT AND COSTLY MAHOGANY BEDROOM SUITE, with

satinwood banding and inlaid vase and floral decoration, comprising:

A 6ft 9in double winged wardrobe, fitted hanging pegs, enclosed by two solid panelled doors, 3ft long, and two short drawers under and recess over with mirror back

A 4ft dressing table fitted 4 drawers and small cupboard, on tapered supports, and surmounted by swing mirror with bevelled plate, 20in by 22in, 2 small side mirrors and 2 jewel drawers

A 4ft washstand with black and variegated marble top, tiled back with bevelled swing mirror and fitted two cupboards and centre recess (marble broken one end)

A 14in enclosed pedestal cupboard *Lenaine £26.0.0*

668   A 2ft 9in handsome and well made mahogany and satin banded Bureau Bookcase in the Sheraton style, fitted three adjustable shelves, enclosed by pair of lattice glazed doors, centre with stationery fitments enclosed by hinged flap and three drawers under *Jenkins £17.0.0*

669   Pair of walnut frame cane chairs *Taylor £1.2.0*

669a   A 24in English early XVIII century decorated Corner Cupboard, enclosed by pair of bent panelled doors with painting of interior scene with figures of courtiers, etc., height 36in *Ford & Co £9.0.0*

❖❖❖❖

1903   Post Horn by C. Kreutzschmann, Dresden, *c* 1800. Diam 6in. Small brass horn with 3 turns, interior of bell painted with gilt flowers on red ground. Original case and crooks *Smalley 15s*

1904   Harpsichord bu Andreas Ruckers, Antwerp, *c* 1630. Length 90in, width 32in. Green painted case with 6 legged stand, gilt. Original instrument with 2 keyboards and 3 stops. Now converted into a piano with 18th century action, one keyboard with ivory naturals and black sharps (imperfect). Front lid painted with classical subjects attributed to Rubens, large lid with dancing scene signed PC (Pieter Codde? 1619 – 1666). Painted soundboard. AR rose. *Greenwood £125.0.0*

1905   Trumpet Marine, German. 16th Century type. Length 71in, width 20in. Pyramidal body enlarged rapidly at base, back 5-sided. Head roughly carved and stamped small pattern. The one string tightened by screw know at top of head. Bridge missing. Said to have been used in a Cistercian monastery. *Smalley £1.7.6*

1906   Banjo, United States of America. Early 19th century. Length 34in, width 11in. Body a wooden hoop with parchment head and 8 screw braces. Neck inlaid with marquetry of coloured woods with bird's head projecting on left side, probably cut out from an earlier piece of Dutch furniture. 6 peg holes; and a

Psaltery, German. 18th century. Length 41in, width 28in. A triangular shaped body terminating in a rudely cut scroll. 2 pierced rosette sound-holes. 22 tuning pins for wire strings. An Irish copper coin dated 1752 inserted in frame. The psaltery, being plucked by the fingers, is the ancestor of the harpsichord. *do £3.15.0*

1907   Mandola, by Joseph Molinari, Venice, 1755. Length 28 ½ in, width 10 ½ in. Lute-shaped body with ebony and ivory inlay. Sunk pasteboard rose. Guitar head with wavy outline and 12 pegs for 6 pairs of strings. Inlaid with mother o' pearl. An interesting instrument in playing order and in its original stamped leather case. *Greenwood £3.15.0*

1908 Cither viol, German. 17th century. Length 28in, width 9in. Pyramidal body, back 5-sided of pinewood. Paper rose. 9 pegs. Scroll broken. The cither-viol was strung with wire strings instead of gut. *Corton 17.6d*

1909 Double Psaltery (Spitz-Harfe), German. 19th century. Length 27in, width 10in. Trapeze shaped body made up of older pieces of wood. Geometrical carving and the letter H with knotted cord and tassels. 12 wire strings on each side of the instrument; and a
Kanoon. Form of Psaltery used in Egypt and other Moslem countries. Derived from Persia. Inlaid with white and black wood. Carved roses. *Yeatman £1.0.0*

1910 Glass harmonica, European *c* 1825. Length 39in. Case of elaborately inlaid coloured woods with star and diamond patterns, the ends with brass and mother o' pearl inlay. The glass plates are now missing. *Taylor 15s*

1923 Harpsichord, by Jacobus and Abraham Kirchmann, London, 1783. Length 8ft, width 38in. Case mahogany with panels; inside satinwood. 2 keyboards. 5 octaves. Ivory naturals, black sharps. 5 stops and machine. 2 pedals for machine and swell flap of cover. 1 K brass perforated rose. A good example of the English double harpsichord still in playable condition. *Ticehurst £135.0.0*

1924 Harpsichord (Clavicombalo), Italian. 16th century. Length 80in, width30in. Instrument of cypress wood removable from its outer case. 2 rows of jacks, 1 keyboard with boxwood keys (naturals) and black sharps. Compass 4 octaves including short octave. Outer case painted green with floral panels and gilt borders. Inside lid paintings of classical subjects. Soundboard with painted flowers (all 17th century work). Stand 17th century. An attractive specimen. *Greenwood £130.0.0*

1925 Piano, by A Pape, Paris. 19th century. Length 5ft 8in, width 2ft 2in. Rectangular case with 6 twisted legs. The whole case gilt, with paintings of Amorini dancing, pastoral scenes, musical instruments and flowers. Within the lid painted trophies of musical instruments and a rural scene. Pedal missing. 5 ½ octaves. An attractive specimen in good condition, by the son of the famous maker H Pape. *do. £145.0.0*

1926 A 24in baton with cameo head ends, tambourine and 2 musette bellows. *Smalley £1.10.0*

1927 Box containing pegs, bridges and other fittings for the repair of old musical instruments. *Hodsdon £1.5.0*

2374 "Venus de Medici", a dolphin at her feet mounted with 2 cupids, 37in high *Malcombe £6.6.0*

2375 Granite circular pedestal with verde marble top, 3ft 4in. *do. £4.4.0*

2376 "Acteon", standing, his right arm raised to his head and his left elbow resting on a tree trunk to which his quiver of arrows is attached, 38in high *Taylor £4.0.0*

2377 Granite circular pedestal with verde marble top, 3ft 4in. high *do.£ 4.4.0*

2378 "Psyche" standing, holding her drapery with her right hand, her hair decked with a diadem of flowers, 31in high *Cuttley £5.10.0*

2379 Verde marble pedestal. 3ft 8in. *Yarrow£ 3.0.0*

2380 "The Proposal", a group of an artist and draped lady standing on circular plinth, 22in high, alabaster *Watson £19.0.0*

2381 Verde marble pedestal. 3ft 8in. *do. £5.0.0*

2382 "Motherless", represented by a girl holding a bird's nest with young, 33in high *Taylor£ 2.10.0*

2383 Sculptured verde marble pedestal with oval top, 4ft. *Yarrow £3.0.0*

2384 "A Girl", standing with drapery to the waist, her left hand resting on a tree trunk, 28in high *Taylor £3.10.0*

2385 Sculptured verde marble pedestal, 4ft. *do. £2.5.0*

2386 Boy, partly draped, holding a bird's nest 27in high *Malcolm £7.0.0*

2387 Granite circular pedestal with verde marble top *Gray £8.0.0*

2388 A Group, "Achilles overpowering a Centaur" 21½ in by 20in (alabaster) *Malcolm £5.0.0*

2389 Spirally fluted verde marble pedestal with revolving top. 3ft 10in. *do. £4.0.0*

2390 A Group, "Achilles and partly draped female", 26in high (alabaster) *Watson £27.0.0*

2391 Spirally fluted verde marble pedestal with revolving top, 3ft 10in. *Watson £5.5.0*

2392 "The Young Apollo", 31in high *Malcolm £6.0.0*

2393 Verde marble circular pedestal. 3ft 4in. *Gray £6.10.0*

2394 "Italian Girl" carrying basket of vine fruit upon her head, 34in high (alabaster) *Yarrow £5.10.0*

2644 A 4ft deal table on stained frame, fitted drawer *Brown 18s*

2645 A 2ft oak vegetable tub and lid *do. 18s*

2646 A refrigerator *do. £4.10.0*

2647 A kitchen wall clock in mahogany circular case *Taylor £1.2.0*

2648 A pair of iron scales and weights, and a small deal meat safe *Brown £1.14.0*

2649 A large copper stock pot and lid with brass tap *Taylor £3.3.0*

2650 A smaller ditto. *do. £2.4.0*

2651 A large copper stewpan and 3 saucepans with lids *Taylor £2.15.0*

2652 A large copper stewpan and lid, 4 ditto saucepans and 3 lids *Brown £2.12.6*

2653 A 12in copper mixing bowl, 2 stewpans and 2 frying pans *do. £2.0.0*

2654 A 13in copper mixing bowl and a 20in fish dish *do. £1.6.0*

2655 A large square copper kettle and lid *do. 16s*

2656 A 17in copper circular preserving pan *do. £1.15.0*

2657 A large copper stewpan and lid, and a 19in preserving pan *do. £1.0.0*

2658 Three copper saucepans, 5 ditto, cake moulds, 4 ditto cake tins 3 ditto measures and 8 ditto odd lids *Muir Mrs £2.6.0*

2659 Six tin trays, 17 cake tins and moulds, various, coffee grinder, mincer, 3 block tin dish covers and 2 plate covers, vegetable press, fish kettle and 4 flat irons *Tanner £1.15.0*

2660 Six tin trays, 17 cake tins, and moulds, various, 6 japanned tin canisters, and a quantity of patty pans, etc. *Daire 10s*

2661 Six japanned tin canisters, sundry cutlery and culinary untensils *Tanner 12s*

2662 Six iron frying pans, iron boiler and sundry iron and enamelled saucepans and frying pans *Brown 9s*

2663 Four enamelled meat trays, ditto washup bowl, sundry enamelled plates and pie dishes and sundry ware pie dishes, and pudding basins *Tanner 10s*

2664 A large earthenware bread crock, and sundries *do. 9s*

❖ ❖ ❖ ❖

Appendix B

Brief details of some families living on Brownsea Island during the van Raalte ownership.

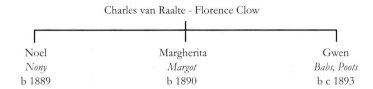

Charles van Raalte - Florence Clow

Noel	Margherita	Gwen
Nony	*Margot*	*Babs, Poots*
b 1889	b 1890	b c 1893

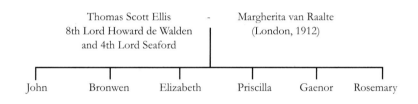

Thomas Scott Ellis
8th Lord Howard de Walden
and 4th Lord Seaford
- Margherita van Raalte
(London, 1912)

John	Bronwen	Elizabeth	Priscilla	Gaenor	Rosemary

❖ ❖ ❖ ❖

Appendix C

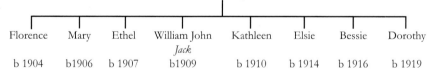

Freeland Battrick - Hannah Hooper (1903, at Parkstone)

Florence	Mary	Ethel	William John	Kathleen	Elsie	Bessie	Dorothy
			Jack				
b 1904	b 1906	b 1907	b 1909	b 1910	b 1914	b 1916	b 1919

Tom Pool and his first wife had a son, Fred, born in 1884; Mrs Pool died at childbirth.

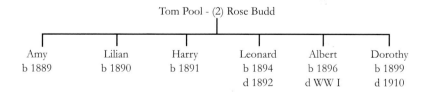

Tom Pool - (2) Rose Budd

Amy	Lilian	Harry	Leonard	Albert	Dorothy
b 1889	b 1890	b 1891	b 1894	b 1896	b 1899
			d 1892	d WW I	d 1910

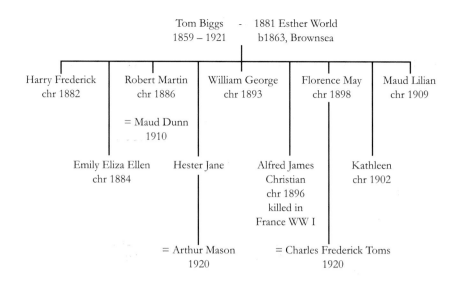

Tom Biggs — 1881 Esther World
1859 – 1921 b1863, Brownsea

Harry Frederick
chr 1882

Robert Martin
chr 1886

= Maud Dunn
1910

William George
chr 1893

Florence May
chr 1898

Maud Lilian
chr 1909

Emily Eliza Ellen
chr 1884

Hester Jane

Alfred James
Christian
chr 1896
killed in
France WW I

Kathleen
chr 1902

= Arthur Mason
1920

= Charles Frederick Toms
1920

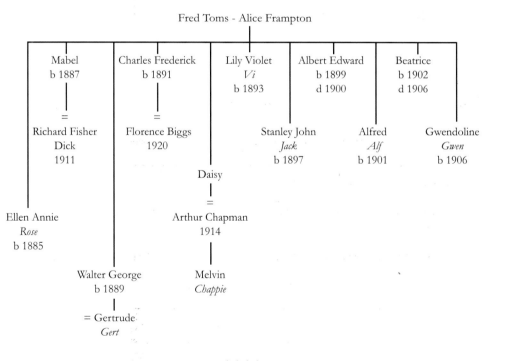

Fred Toms - Alice Frampton

Mabel
b 1887

Charles Frederick
b 1891

Lily Violet
Vi
b 1893

Albert Edward
b 1899
d 1900

Beatrice
b 1902
d 1906

=

Richard Fisher
Dick
1911

=

Florence Biggs
1920

Stanley John
Jack
b 1897

Alfred
Alf
b 1901

Gwendoline
Gwen
b 1906

Daisy

=

Ellen Annie
Rose
b 1885

Arthur Chapman
1914

Walter George
b 1889

Melvin
Chappie

= Gertrude
Gert

❖ ❖ ❖ ❖

87

INDEX

S

T

V

W